# SEEKING PALESTINE

New Palestinian Writing
on Exile and Home

# SEEKING PALESTINE

## New Palestinian Writing on Exile and Home

EDITED BY PENNY JOHNSON AND RAJA SHEHADEH

OLIVE
BRANCH
PRESS

An imprint of Interlink Publishing Group, Inc.
**www.interlinkbooks.com**

First American edition published in 2013 by

OLIVE BRANCH PRESS
An imprint of Interlink Publishing Group, Inc.
46 Crosby Street
Northampton, Massachusetts 01060
www.interlinkbooks.com

Library of Congress Cataloging-in-Publication Data available

ISBN 978-1-56656-906-4

Images on pages 2-3, 72-73, 150-51: Emily Jacir
*Where We Come From* 2001-2003 (three details)
American passport, 30 texts, 32 c-prints and 1 video
Copyright: Emily Jacir
Courtesy of Alexander and Bonin, New York

Cover photograph: Raeda Sa'adeh

Printed and bound in the United States of America

To order our free 52-page, full-color catalog, call us at
1-800-238-LINK or visit www.interlinkbooks.com

# Acknowledgement

A special thanks to the Palestine Festival of Literature (Palfest) where the idea of this book was born, in one of the many wonderful encounters Palfest fosters between international writers, editors and publishers, and their Palestinian counterparts. The editors of *Seeking Palestine* are pleased to dedicate their royalties to Palfest, as a small contribution to continuing the conversation and breaking the barriers.

# Contents

CONTENTS

# PENNY JOHNSON

# Introduction:
# Neither Homeland nor Exile
# are Words

In this volume, historian Beshara Doumani recalls a
song from World War II Haifa—a song that Doumani cannot place
in any archive, even though he possesses two almost translucent
pieces of paper with the ditty scrawled in his own childish handwriting. Indeed, he can sing this sailor's song—and it only—in an
accent from a vanished Haifa neighborhood. It is not nostalgia, but
wonder and questioning that inform his reflections. In an encounter
between memory and imagination, a rootless memory becomes a
miracle of "immaculate birth."

Writing outside the archives, new Palestinian writing on exile
and home asks questions laced with wonder. How do Palestinians
live, imagine and think about home and exile six decades after
the dismemberment of historic Palestine and in the complicated
present tense of a truncated and transitory Palestine? What
happens when the "idea of Palestine" that animated so many around
the globe becomes an "Authority" and Palestine a patchwork of
divided territory? When we, my co-editor Raja Shehadeh and I,
asked Palestinian essayists, novelists, poets and critics to respond,
we found ourselves on new ground—fascinating, intimate and provocative. And it seemed very much like our writers were conversing
with each other—and with Palestinian writers before them—ex-
changing memories, reflections, an occasional joke or a poignant

moment of sorrow, like friends on a summer night in the cool hills of Palestine or at the corner café in New York or on the terrace over the sea in Beirut. Wherever they were, the tone was convivial, the talk exhilarating, and the memories unconventional, both personal and worldly. *Seeking Palestine*, then, is not a representative anthology— this was neither the editors' intention nor their aptitude; for an excellent anthology of Palestinian writing until the early 1990s, the reader should turn to Salma Khadra Jayyusi's magisterial *Anthology of Modern Palestinian Writing*. Our book is in an intimate key and its claim is to imagine, rather than represent.

Indeed, our writers sidestep representation and imaginatively affirm new ways of being Palestinian, giving their own resonating and contemplative answers to the world's stock questions. By now, the treacherous politics of representation are perhaps all too familiar. But the terrain of imagination and memory, which this anthology's writers navigate with elegance and sensitivity, is also potent, though perilous. Even as they recognize memory's function as a means of resistance and of belonging, our writers avoid the obvious trap of nostalgic memory and are aware that memory-as-reclamation is a vexed project: as the novelist Mischa Hiller points out, when the exiled and dispossessed "remember" Palestine, whether experienced or imagined, their memories might seem quite alien (and alienating) to the Palestinians who live there now.

While Doumani seeks to transform his "miracle memory" into a "mortal" one—one that can be forgotten, with all the privileges of security that such forgetting implies—Suad Amiry fights against memories, those iconic images that have haunted Palestinians for over sixty years since the 1948 Nakba when Palestine was dismembered. Her words are a drumbeat of "No"es addressed to her obsession, Palestine. She writes:

> And it would not be about the blooming almond trees and the red flowering pomegranates that were *not* tenderly picked in the spring of 1948 nor in the summer after.

But Amiry's roll-call of insistent noes, like a photo negative, both reverses and preserves these inescapable images. And, in fact, her prose-poem is inspired by a telling phrase of Mahmoud Darwish's that heads one of this volume's sections: "my country: close to me as my prison."[1] And her denial of the memory of almond trees perhaps brings their blooming even more persistently into the imagination. Darwish's evocation of blossoming almonds in a late poem written from his "exile" in Ramallah comes to mind:

Neither homeland nor exile are words,
But passions of whiteness in a
Description of the almond blossom...

If a writer were to compose a successful piece
Describing an almond blossom, the fog would rise
From the hills, and people, all the people, would say:
This is it.
These are the words of our national anthem.

The writers here also refuse homeland and exile as mere words, and search for ways—images, fragments, memories—to lift the fog from the hills. Raja Shehadeh peers through a "gossamer veil" of white fog on a 2003 visit to the Israeli-bombed ruins of the Muqataa, at once the current seat of the Palestinian Authority, the past Israeli military headquarters in Ramallah, and a former British Mandate police fortress. In three diary entries of an "internal exile," he ponders the "layers of meaning" of this site and wonders when "Palestine/Israel [will] come to mean nothing more to their people than home."

Politically besieged as it is, Palestine evokes a particular obligation of belonging in its far-flung "inhabitants" for whom insistent memory becomes a mode of habitation. Like Shehadeh, several writers speak of a desire to move beyond this particular kind of identification, to where a robust Palestine can be "nothing more... than home." Reflecting on the ties that bind him to a country he has never seen, Hiller searches for something "bigger-hearted and more inclusive" than just a state—"the golden thread that not just ties us back to Palestine but *pulls us forward* to a new one." Hiller thus seeks Palestine not simply in a political entity but in an inclusive vision of Palestine and Palestinian identity; he also shares with Raja Shehadeh a wish for Palestine to be a place that can be home or not, a Palestine that is a *choice*:

> We are already reimagining a Palestine that reflects who we are now and who we hope to become.

For poet and essayist Sharif Elmusa, the fragment of memory is the broken blackboard where his American-born children write their names in a long-deferred visit to his ruined school in a destroyed refugee camp near Jericho. In his powerful memoir, the "backpack of contradictions" that is his self moves among worlds and identities, subject to flashes of memory, where the "refugee camp ambushes me anywhere, any moment." A supermarket visit, for example:

> Marveling today at the Safeway's abundance
> of tuna fish cans,
> I remember my friend Hussein.
> He was the genius of the school.
> He breathed in history, grammar, math
> as easily as he breathed the dust of the camp.

A memory of a tuna fish can, stolen by the hungry child she was in a Jerusalem orphanage, leads novelist Susan Abulhawa to a searing account of her childhood odyssey back and forth from Palestine, Kuwait, Jordan and the US, passed along among parents, relatives and foster homes; she is indeed a child Odysseus passing through borders without papers or protection, armed only with her intelligence and resilience. Hers is a story of Palestinian identity and survival that is made up not of iconic images, but broken fragments heroically pieced together. Her Palestinian "inheritance" of people, experiences and memory is also, in its narration, her Palestinian "triumph."

Lila-Abu Lughod writes, in her memoir of her activist father, Ibrahim, and her own "political education," that Palestine at first resided for her in relatives, food, and an accent she only later realized was from the costal city of Jaffa. But she adds:

> ...even if I had not had these childhood tastes and memories of family, there would still be no way not to be drafted into being Palestinian.

And Jean Said Makdisi, writing from a mountain village in Lebanon, asks, "[w]hat am I without Palestine? And what is Palestine without me?" Distrustful of nationalism, she remains, like Suad Amiry, obsessed with, possessed by, Palestine. During the long Lebanese civil war, Palestine returns in a domestic detail:

> Repair and restoration are constant elements in my life. During the war, I could not bear a torn curtain, a broken window or a hole in the wall left by shrapnel: I was constantly fixing, repairing, painting...I am sure this is an aspect of my Palestinian history.

Said Makdisi's lost homeland is Jerusalem, at once an "ancient epicenter of civilization" and of "present-day violence and wickedness"—but always, in her imagination, grand. Rema Hammami's Jerusalem, in her poignant and sometimes hilarious account of her decaying neighborhood of Sheikh Jarrah, is a place of a genteel past and a paralyzed present. Its "shrine-keepers" are elderly Palestinian ladies, the "Miss Havishams," left behind by migratory families in their decaying mansions—until the Mossad, Israel's spy agency, moves into the neighborhood and a well-funded and government-supported movement of settlers begins a relentless campaign of dispossession.

Hammami takes us through the Occupation, two intifadas, and a neverending peace process with a vivid cast of characters whose resilience gives them more than a family resemblance to the hero of poet Mourid Barghouti's tale, Mahmoud the driver. On the day Israel invades Palestinian towns in the West Bank in 2002, Mahmoud is determined to drive his passengers from

Ramallah to the bridge crossing to Jordan. He will drive any route to fulfil his mission, whether through fields, muddy waterholes, or around checkpoints. Barghouti observes:

> We are now his nation: an old man and two women (one of whom doesn't cover her hair and face, while the other wears a full veil); a man who's short and another who's fat; a university student; and a poet who is amazed by everything he sees and doesn't want to spoil it by talking.

A nation, Mahmoud-style, is created and preserved in the crowded space of a service taxi traveling through an insecure and hostile space which negates that very nation. The moving taxi becomes a homeland with the poet as witness.

In one of Adania Shibli's lyrical trio of stories, she encounters little girls in the ravaged Jenin refugee camp, their eyes flashing as they demand entry to a reading she is about to give at the Jenin Freedom Theater. Their spirit restores Shibli to Jenin, the city of her childhood, and to herself. In another story, Shibli contemplates her "little watch" that gives her a strange sense of time while she is in Palestine—including, quite comfortingly, reducing the hours of a search and interrogation at Israel's Ben Gurion Airport to zero. Rana Barakat, a historian at Birzeit University writing from Chicago after being denied entry to Palestine, finds herself suspended between home and exile:

> The ties that bind me to myself were all undone when an anonymous official announced in an all-too-ordinary tone that I would not be allowed to enter *here* and would subsequently be deported from *here*. Born in exile, living in exile, or returning to exile—I was not sure where to place myself.

Visual artist Emily Jacir utilized her "place" as a Palestinian with an American passport to access Palestine for Palestinians who are forbidden entry. In the three images from her powerful 2001–03 series, *Where We Come From,* that open each section of *Seeking Palestine,* Jacir meticulously fulfils a request from a Palestinian who cannot enter Palestine or whose movement is restricted therein. It is an intimate visual—and physical—intervention into the stasis of exile and the ongoing process of fragmenting Palestine.

Karma Nabulsi describes exile as a lost time, where Palestinians are separated from their own revolutionary history. From the "generation of revolution" herself, Nabulsi vividly describes the paralysis in Palestinian politics in an era where liberation struggles seem to be off the agenda:

> Everyone else has moved on. In a world whose intellectual framework is derived from university courses in postcolonial or cultural studies, from the discourse of post-nationalism or human rights or global governance, from post-conflict and security literature, the Palestinians are stuck fast in historical amber. They can't move on, and the language that could assist them to do so is as extinct as Aramaic.

Attending the funeral of a PLO activist in Beirut who had retained, against all odds, his revolutionary spirit, Nabulsi feels, "something...[is] about to give." This sense of stirrings, whether of a new language to imagine the idea of Palestine, of the resurgence of resistance, or the reconfiguration of exile and home, is a current running through the reflections of a number of our writers. For Nabulsi, the possibility of a revolutionary renewal is encouraged by the Arab Spring; for poet Fady Joudah, the possibility of a "Palestine that never was" emerges in the mathematics of the imagination. In a preface to his five poems, he writes:

> Perhaps that Palestine that never was is true to exile as a state of being; not exile as a state of despair or eternal longing, but a state where one is free to wander the earth between the possible and the necessary return, since what has not yet arrived has not yet been lost.

It is telling that we considered two working titles for this volume that seem to be contradictory: "After Palestine" and "Beginning Palestine." (Our very first title, "Exile's Antinomies," borrowing Edward Said's notion of exile's irreducible contradictions from his seminal essay, "Reflections on Exile," would have been rejected by any canny publisher.) We considered "After Palestine" in its multiple senses, whether after post-Oslo Palestine, after the loss of historic Palestine or indeed simply, as our title now claims, seeking Palestine. But "Beginning Palestine" also spoke to the purpose of our enterprise and to the imaginations of our writers. Edward Said (once again) makes the useful distinction between "origins" and "beginnings." Rather than looking backward to a fixed point of origin, beginnings are a "first step in the intentional production of meaning."[2] Perhaps then, in the complicated circumstances of "after Palestine" in which Palestinians and Palestine are entangled, it is time to seek—and write—Palestine as a beginning.

*Ramallah, January 2012*

**Notes**

[1] The titles of this anthology's first two sections are taken from a relatively early poem by Mahmoud Darwish, *Poem of the Land*, and the third from one of his late poems, *With the Fog so Dense on the Bridge*. Darwish's understanding of the interplay of distance and closeness, exile and home, although always evident, became more pronounced as he lived an internal exile in Ramallah in his latter years.

[2] Edward W. Said, *Beginnings: Intention and Method* (New York: Columbia University Press, 1975).

# EXILE/HOME

My Country:
Distant as My Heart from Me

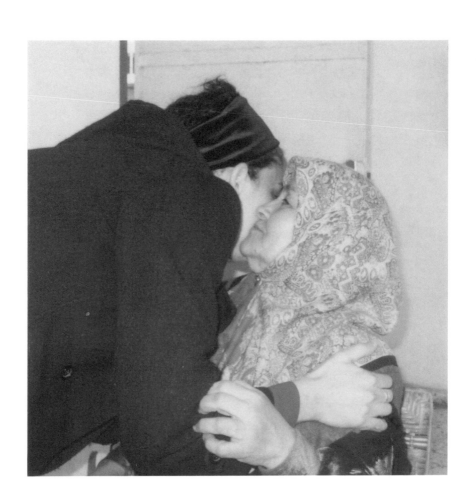

Visit my mother, hug and kiss her and
tell her that these are from her son.
Visit the sea at sunset and smell it for
me and walk a little bit......enough.
Am I greedy?

I have a Gazan I.D. so I should be in Gaza. I
left Gaza for Ramallah in 1995 and cannot
go back. I also cannot move to any place in
the West Bank because of the Israeli
restrictions. The Israelis refused to give me a
West Bank I.D. because, as they claim, for
"security reasons"!

- Jihad
Born in Shati Refugee Camp, Gaza City
Living in Ramallah
Gazan I.D. card
Father and Mother from Asdud
(exiled in 1948)

Notes: We sat together and drank coffee and tea while she
asked all about Jihad, his wife and kids. We also talked about
the intifada and its effect on everyone. When I was leaving, she
put two handfuls of sweets in my handbag to bring back to
Jihad.

زوري أمي و عانقيها و قبليها، و أخبريها
أن كل هذا من ابنها، و زوري البحر وقت
الغروب و تنشقي رائحته نيابةً عني
و تمشي قليلا...وكفى. هل أنا طمّاع؟

هويتي غزاوية و لذلك يتوجب عليّ أن أكون
في غزّة. لقد غادرت غزّة إلى رام الله عام ١٩٩٥
و لا أستطيع العودة، كما لا أستطيع الانتقال إلى
أي مكان آخر في الضفة الغربية بسبب القيود
الإسرائيلية. لقد رفض الإسرائيليون منحي
هوية ضفةٍ غربية بحجة أسباب "أمنية"!

- جهاد
من مواليد مخيم الشاطئ للاجئين، مدينة غزة
يعيش في رام الله
هوية غزّة
الأب و الأم من أسدود
(نفيا عام ١٩٤٨)

ملاحظات: لقد جلسنا و شربنا القهوة و الشاي معا فيما كانت
أمه تسأل عن أحوال جهاد وزوجته و أولاده و قد تحدثنا عن
الانتفاضة و أثرها على الجميع، و حينما كنت استعد للمغادرة
و ضعت حفنتين من الحلوى في حقيبتي لكي أعطيهما لجهاد.

# SUSAN ABULHAWA

# Memories of an Un-Palestinian Story, in a Can of Tuna

I was a thief.

Um Hasan, our kind-hearted cook, didn't give me the tuna. I'm sure, because she'd have also given me something to open it with. But there I was with my stolen can of tuna that evening, hiding out in one of the empty classrooms. It was 1982 or 1983 at Dar al-Tifl al-Arabi, an orphanage for girls in East Jerusalem. It was getting late. In that corner of memory, the sky was grey-blue and we were already locked in for the night. We weren't supposed to be in the classrooms after school hours. And, conversely, we weren't allowed in the dormitories during the day when school was in session. When the classes were open, the dorms were closed, and vice versa.

I might have told myself that Um Hasan would have given the tuna to me had I asked because she often gave me contraband cheese sandwiches. The first time she did that was after she saw me staring at two of the day-students, girls who went back to a home after school. They had families waiting for them at the end of classes. I imagined a loving mother, anxious for her daughter's return, who would embrace her child and proceed to do mother-daughter things that were suffused with laughter, cuddles, books, cooking and unimaginable joy. The father I imagined, equally magnificent, would look at his daughter with complete adoration and pride. I stared at those day-students, holding back my disgust that their fathers could be proud of them with the low grades they brought home. I always got the highest marks in class. A father like that would really have been proud of me. I imagined the food they ate—delicious, warm, hearty and with real meat.

"Come with me, girl," Um Hasan said, surprising me as envy seeped from my pores while I waited for the day-students to finish their sandwiches and leave, so I could pick up their discarded crusts.

I assumed Um Hasan had peeked into my wicked thoughts about those girls, but I went with her because I always did as I was told, which was another reason I was the one who deserved a good family that loved me. I had good grades and I was obedient. (The matter of stealing tuna was unknown and should not count against me on the list of my traits.)

I followed Um Hasan to the main dormitory building, where she made me wait in the hallway while she went into the kitchen. A few minutes later she stepped out, a hand behind her back, and looked around to see if anyone was watching before she handed me half a pita sandwich with cheese spread and cucumber. "I'll make you more whenever you want. You don't need to eat anybody's scraps, girl."

There wasn't enough food for Um Hasan to do that for every girl, so she singled out a few of us for clandestine snacks. She picked the runts, the ones who likely couldn't fend for themselves, or those of us who were clearly hungry and undernourished and, importantly, those of us who wouldn't tattle and make her lose her job.

I never squealed on anyone—a virtue I added to my list in three parts, to make the list longer: Never Tattle, Never Squeal, Keeper of Secrets.

As I tried to open the can by beating a fork into it with a rock, smelly tuna water leaked and squirted out all over my hands and clothes. That was my condition when I heard one of the girls running down the hall, calling my name. She stopped when she saw me and said, "There you are! You'd better hurry up back to the dorm. Sitt Hidaya sent word for you to go see Sitt Hind." Dread washed over me. My heart started beating so hard I thought it would jump out of my chest.

5

I must have frozen because she continued, "Susie, you'd really better come before Sitt Hidaya finds out you're in here."

Her words calmed me a little. Sitt Hidaya apparently didn't know that I was not in the dorm and therefore she probably didn't know about the tuna either. But had I heard correctly that Sitt Hind wanted to see me? She had never asked to see me. Sitt Hind was the founder of the orphanage and rarely had time for the everyday details of our lives. She was always so busy traveling to raise money for the orphanage that I didn't think she asked to see any of us. In fact, I didn't realize she even knew my name.

"Why does Sitt Hind want to see me? Did she say *my* name? Susie?" I asked.

"How would I know, dumbass? I'm here saving your life from Sitt Hidaya. If she ever finds out what you're doing, she'll kill you and feed you to the donkeys. You should be thanking me and running quick to see Sitt Hind instead of asking stupid questions," she snapped and left.

I shoved aside the as yet unopened, badly battered can of tuna and ran behind her. She went back to the dorm and I headed downstairs, towards the black iron door that was always locked at that hour. I had no idea how I would get out to see Sitt Hind in her home, which was just a few steps from our building.

The door opened as I approached it. Espi, my friend who was several years older than me, held it open. Espi was the unofficial police. She possessed the trust and confidence of the administrators, as well as the keys to nearly every door in the school. And we accepted Espi's authority without question, partly because of her access to all the keys.

As Espi turned to lock the door behind me, I wondered if I was going to be let back in. I grew worried, but still I hurried toward Sitt Hind's home, climbed up the stairs and knocked on her door.

Then it hit me how badly I reeked of tuna.

I hadn't even had the sense or time to wash my hands, so I just stood there when Sitt Hind opened the door and asked me to come in. She seemed so old and frail—as most adults with grey hair seem to children. Looking back, she must have been only in her fifties. She was thin, with slightly sunken cheeks and short hair cut in a tidy bob. Time, war and military occupation had sharpened her eyes and set them deep in her face. The lines on her skin spoke of dignity and a tortured heart. She was always well-dressed; even on that evening, alone in her own home, she wore a simple below-the-knees skirt and an elegant blouse. She was like a god and I was afraid she'd smell the stench on me when I passed by. I stood in her doorway too long, looking at her, contemplating my predicament. But eventually I had to make a move, so I rushed in and stood far from her. My fists were clenched to hold in the stench on my hands. But I could still smell it and it grew stronger the more I thought about it. Why hadn't I just stopped at a sink to wash my hands? Now I couldn't even shake Sitt Hind's hand, much less accept her hug when she came towards me with open arms. I just backed away. I was so ashamed of smelling so bad.

I will never know the real reason why Sitt Hind called me to her home that evening. Perhaps it was to get to know me better since I was excelling in all my classes and stood out among my peers. She asked how I was doing. She asked me about Ameena, her one-time ward who had grown into the woman who gave birth to me.

Ameena and two of her younger sisters, my aunts, had lived at Dar al-Tifl many years before I was born. It wasn't often that a second generation came to Dar al-Tifl, especially when it came to a bright student, which my mother had been. Maybe Sitt Hind was curious to know what happened to her former pupil. She had educated, fed and clothed my mother and aunts when my grandfather died and my illiterate grandmother had to go off to Kuwait to work as a maid for a sheikha there. As she often did for girls who showed promise, Sitt Hind sought scholarships for them to study abroad. My mother ended up going to Germany to study nursing. That's where she was when Israel took the rest of Palestine, including Jerusalem, in the 1967 war. So my mother was never able to return home and went to

Kuwait instead, where Palestinian refugees flocked as cheap labor. I don't know if Ameena was ever in touch with Sitt Hind after that. I doubt it. I don't think Sitt Hind knew anything about her until I, Ameena's firstborn, arrived at the orphanage doorsteps thirteen years later.

But the desert winds of the Arab world always arrive with news and rumors. Gossip is a staple of our society and my mother provided good fodder for it. That's one thing I inherited from her. Maybe Sitt Hind knew that my mother was remarried and living comfortably in Kuwait. She probably even knew that my mother had abandoned me in the United States as an infant and then came back for me when I was five years old. I was living with my uncle in what others often described as a white trash neighborhood of Charlotte, North Carolina. My uncle's wife, Mary, was the first of several women I called Mama. She was an Evangelical Christian and had raised me until then on the fire-and-brimstone television sermons of Jim Bakker and Jerry Falwell.

I think Mary was the first person to call me Susie, a nickname that is more my name than any of the other names on my official documents. She worked behind the food counter at K-Mart and one of the great joys of my life then was the privilege of knowing which inflated balloon contained the blue card that entitled its owner to a free meal. I simply paid five cents, picked the secret balloon and won a free lunch when I popped it. I acted surprised each time so Mama wouldn't get in trouble. My other great joy was my pride in being the only kid who got to ride on the side of the garbage truck alongside my uncle every other Thursday when it came to our street for trash pickup. My uncle looked so important in his official blue one-piece uniform, filthy with the remnants of other people's garbage.

Those early years in the US ensured that I would speak English with a southern American accent, which would, many years later, help me pull off an Oscar-worthy act that got me into the country at the age of thirteen, alone, without a passport or a green card. I got into the US on the strength of that perfect accent, the kind hearts of two immigration officers, the winning smile of a child, and the cunning of a survivor.

I'm sure Sitt Hind knew that after I met my mother at the age of five, she took me back with her to Kuwait and left me to live with my grandmother. Ameena visited, but mostly she was in Saudi Arabia, working as a nurse, living in a dormitory with the other imported labor. Eventually, she remarried.

I don't know what tall tale my grandmother told Sitt Hind to justify my living at Dar al-Tifl when my mother could clearly afford to care for me, especially since her new husband was an important person in Kuwait with a lot of stars on his army uniform. I'm sure my grandmother told a convincing story. And I'm sure no one knew the truth (not all of it anyway) because it would be at least another twenty years before I would ever tell another human being that the man my mother married had already molested me when I was seven years old, long before she married him. It would be at least twenty-five years before I would admit to anyone that at the age of eight, when my mother married my molester, I became my stepfather's mistress.

Until I burned down their home.

His reaction to the fire was proof that I was the problem. People extolled his self-control and patience for not giving me the good beating I deserved, and they criticized him for the same reason. They said he must be a saint to put up with a troublemaker like me who wasn't even his daughter. They said my mother was lucky to have found such a man. "He didn't even yell at the girl," a woman said. And she was right.

My stepfather never said a word to me on the matter. But, in the soot of memory, our eyes locked one day and he held me in a terrifying stare that immobilized me until he looked away, an eternity later. It was a stare swollen with a secret rage that I could only interpret through my adult eyes, many years later. He had wanted to unleash his fury for the financial loss I had caused. He wanted to pound me, maybe rape me and rip me to shreds. But doing so would risk another irrational act on my part, which could have destroyed him. I suppose he didn't understand that I would not have squealed, not because I was a Keeper of Secrets, but because I felt culpable.

The fire was an accident, but maybe there are no accidents. Maybe the accusations I got from everyone around me were correct—that I was jealous of my mother's marriage and wanted to destroy it. Maybe I just wanted to burn the scenery of my life. Maybe, at the age of nine, I needed my world to smoulder on the outside like it was smouldering inside. Things need to match up when you're young. They make more sense that way. Maybe. And maybe I knew that the traits that really counted—Unworthy, Dirty, Bad—far outweighed the other entries on my list.

So I was sent away.

Like the times before, I do not recall the details of this abandonment. My memory moves from the grip of my stepfather's stare after the fire, to being in Jordan with a relative, too embarrassed to let anyone know that I had only one pair of panties that I wore and washed at the sink every so often, under the cover of night when the world was sleeping.

I went from one relative to another. In one home, mosquitoes left my legs looking like I had chicken pox. Someone told me that I must have sweet blood since mosquitoes had not dotted ugly welts on anyone else's legs. I liked the idea that my blood was sweeter than most and I secretly thought it probably gave me special powers. But I didn't add that to my list, since I wasn't yet sure what my powers were.

After a few months, school started but I was not to attend. I was without papers, without a passport. I didn't belong anywhere but to a political discussion called "The Question of Palestine." I was an abstraction. I was nothing. And, for the first time in my life, faced with my greatest fear of being denied an education, I became unruly and defiant and loud and openly hostile and angry and erratic and moody. "Good grades" was the only consistent entry on my list of virtues and I couldn't bear losing my life's only constant. So I pleaded and panicked and cried and screamed and bothered everyone around me until the pity and charity I had been shown dried up.

Finally, my grandmother arrived from Kuwait. She had brought a suitcase of clothes for me, with several sets of underwear, and she showed me how to sneak into the West Bank through the Allenby Bridge. That's an impossible feat now, but things were different in 1980. Today's technology was absent then and the crossing was mayhem: an open space with suitcases splayed open, soldiers rummaging through them, children running around. I was told to "stay with that family over there with all the kids." I did as I was told. Having been promised schooling, I had gone back to being my obedient self and restored that attribute to my list.

There seemed to be hundreds of kids in that family. In reality, there were probably some twenty siblings and cousins with their parents, and I could simply blend in or hide among them. p. 28 (15) Being shorter than average may have saved me that day, as I could easily be invisible in the shuffle. "I'll meet you on the other side," my grandmother said and began reciting verses from the Quran. She instructed me not to look any soldier in the eye, not to try to find her, and to recite the *Fatiha* and every other verse from the Quran that I had memorized, over and over in my mind, until I made it across. I obeyed. I knew a lot of Quran verses by heart. (That, too, was on my list of virtues.)

I stayed with the large family. I stripped off my clothes and stood in my panties, in a line with all the other women and girls standing against the wall as the Israeli soldier took away our shoes in crates and came back an eternity later, pouring the inspected shoes into a pile on the floor. Still reciting the *Fatiha* to myself, I waited for the adults to move. They waited for the soldier's nod. Then we all fell to our knees around the pile to retrieve our shoes. That's all I remember. I must have met up with my grandmother on the other side. She probably paid the women of the large family for playing along. She must have taken me to Dar al-Tifl. And I must have said goodbye.

"Fine," I answered when Sitt Hind asked me how my mother was doing, but all I could think about was whether or not she could smell the tuna all over me. Worse, I began to worry that I was stinking up her house and that the smell would linger long after I was gone. I didn't tell her, nor would I have even if I had not been stinky, that Ameena had not tried to contact me at all since I had arrived at Dar al-Tifl nearly two years earlier.

Because I was a Keeper of Secrets. I Never Squealed. I Never Tattled. And, on the matter of being abandoned, I would never have tattled on my mother—not even to myself, in the privacy of my own thoughts.

Sitt Hind might have been disappointed in Ameena. Maybe she was disappointed in me, too, on account of how strangely I was acting. That thought still bothers me. It bothers me that I never got a chance to demonstrate to Sitt Hind that I was worth her investment; that I had internalized her commitment to invest and believe in the humanity and potential of others; that I treasured the education she gave me and would do the best I could with it; that I loved her for it and wanted desperately to hug her that day; and that I would never be the kind of mother who sacrificed or abandoned her daughter.

I would never get a chance to express any of that to Sitt Hind. The evening I stood reeking of tuna in her home was the last time I ever saw her. Sometime after, I was given the traumatic news that I would be leaving Dar al-Tifl. My father had sent for me to live with him in the United States.

Thirty years later, just two weeks ago, I watched a film that depicts the life of Sitt Hind. There is a scene in which Sitt Hind gives one of her girls the choice to stay at Dar al-Tifl or go with her father who wants to marry her off. The girl asks to stay and Sitt Hind ensures that this happens, against the wishes of the girl's father. It occurred to me in the theater that perhaps Sitt Hind had summoned me that evening so many years ago to ask if I wanted to go and live with my father, because she was prepared to keep me if I didn't. I wish I could remember our brief conversation. Maybe she did ask me. I might have been agreeable to going, not believing it possible that I would ever leave the orphanage otherwise. I just don't remember. And I suppose it doesn't matter.

So I came to the US at the age of thirteen. At the age of fourteen, after a year of going to school with bruises, black eyes and broken bones, I became a ward of the Mecklenberg County Court in North Carolina, got a green card, and my father was convicted of misdemeanor child abuse. Several foster homes later, Social Services settled me in a Southern Baptist children's home—Mill's Home. I was one of two kids on that campus who was not Christian. The other kid, Alan, was Jewish, and he and I formed a friendship based on a common annoyance at their endless efforts to convert us.

Alan was prudent and patient. I was impulsive and foolhardy, and when the possibility of family and belonging was dangled in front of me—my greatest and most incessant want—I would leap for it without thought or care. So when I reached out to Ameena and she invited me to visit, I wasn't going to let a technicality get in my way. As a ward of the court, I couldn't leave US jurisdition before the age of eighteen. But I used my resourcefulness and cunning to leap for the great carrot. I found a way to leave at the age of seventeen and spent a week in Kuwait visiting Ameena, who had just given birth to my fifth and youngest half sister. For a week's visit with my birth mother, I gave up the financial security of being a ward of the court, which would have provided for me and paid for my education until I graduated. Upon my return to Thomasville to finish my senior year living on my own, I learned that I couldn't sustain myself working at Burger King and Mr. Gatti's Pizza. My homeroom teacher, Anne, took me in, and I finished high school living with her, got a scholarship for college, and then for graduate school. Anne didn't believe in God.

That's how I went from immersion in Evangelical Christianity for the first few years of my life to conservative Islam through early adolescence, to Southern Baptist Christianity and then atheism through high school. Before the age of sixteen, I had lived in twenty-one different homes, only two of which were with either of my parents. The rest were with relatives, in foster care or at institutions. I have lived and traveled all over the world, but my heart has never left Jerusalem, where all my ancestors are buried, where Sitt Hind showed me that I was worthy, and where Um Hasan told me that I didn't need to wait for anyone's scraps. I abused my own body with food and drugs to find some measure of control. I fell in love and, alone, gave birth to the love of my life. I've had a broken heart. A broken body. And, at times, a broken everything.

Through it all, I've kept an old photo of Atiyeh, my grandfather, taken perhaps in the 1920s. He's wearing a Palestinian *galabiya* with a *tarboush* on his head, a sign of importance that the Turks left behind in Palestine. His moustache is thick and long and curled upward at the tips. He is standing erect, his chest puffed out as if holding his breath. I am told that he was a strong and stern man. He was stubborn, persistent, and never backed down from a fight. He did not accept weakness from his sons and was especially hard on his youngest son, the man who would become my father. My grandfather lived his whole life in al-Tur on the Mount of Olives in Palestine, where our family is rooted for at least nine hundred years. He inherited very large plots of land on that fabled hill overlooking Jerusalem. And he died before he could ever imagine that nearly everything he had would be taken away and all his sons would be forced into exile, denied their right to return home.

My life is very far from the destiny that Atiyeh thought he was bequeathing to his descendants. This daughter of a long line of a huge clan of Palestinian farmers grew up alone, fending for herself, so far away from her birthright. My life is also very far from the experience of most Palestinian women in the world, who are almost always surrounded and protected by large families.

Mine has been an un-Palestinian life. Yet I have come to understand that it represents the most basic truth about what it means to be Palestinian—dispossessed, disinherited and exiled; and what it ultimately means to resist. That truth is this:

To be alone, without papers, without a family or a clan, a land or a country means that one must live at the mercy of others. There are those who might take pity on you and those who will exploit and harm you. You live at the whims of your hosts, sometimes preyed upon and nearly always put in your place. Rarely are you treated with the dignity of an equal, until you demand and fight for it. But there are particular beauties and peculiar strengths that can only be found in the trenches of such a life—like the ability to hold your head high, even when someone has their boot on your neck; the wisdom to do whatever it takes to get an education, even when you're denied a school; the freedom of shedding shame and living one's truth, no matter how messy, without apologies; the marvel of a body that heals itself from the intentional harm of others and rises to rebuild; and the victory of a heart that does not succumb to fear or hatred or bitterness.

The thing about being an adult is that you eventually stop needing things to match up and you manage, somehow, when your birthright or your dreams don't coincide with your destiny. Though I was denied my home and heritage, I had the great fortune to claim my inheritance of Atiyeh's stubbornness and his attachment to and love of the land; of Sitt Hind's wisdom and generosity; and of Um Hasan's gentle heart. These have been the stuff of my Palestinian identity. My stories are the stuff of my intifada. And every reader is part of my triumph.

# BESHARA DOUMANI

## A Song from Haifa

| | |
|---|---|
| *Tsipora ya nour el-ain* | Tiaspora, light of the eye |
| *Kanteenik saffani fain?* | Where has your Canteen gotten me? |
| *Badrob idi 'ala jaybtain* | I slap both my pockets |
| *Ma bala'i irsh yjawibni!* | But not a piastre answers me |
| | |
| *Marrah kunit fil kanteen* | Once, I was in the Canteen |
| *Wa min tafari ba-sib el-deen* | Broke and cursing God |
| *Willa ajani dabit tkheen* | When a burly Officer grabbed me |
| *W'alli imshi uddami* | And marched me away |
| *Akhadni 'al ga-rid room* | He threw me in the Guard Room |
| *W'alli a'tini basak ya mal'oun* | And said: "Hand over your pass, you ass" |
| | |
| *Lamma akhad el-bas: Ya sh-hari* | Oh! What a black day |
| *Surit altim 'ala hali* | To take my pass away |
| *Akhad riz-it 'ayyali* | I pounded my head and screamed |
| *Wa man'ani roht el-kanteen* | He ruined my family's livelihood |
| | And forbade me from the Canteen |
| | |
| *Wa shway jayyini el-shaweesh* | Soon after, the Sergeant yelled at me |
| *Wa alli fenak ya iblees?* | "You devil! Where have you been? |
| *Marra bi-tkun uddami* | One second, you're here before me |
| *bi-truh turkud zay el-exebrees* | The next, you bolt like an express train |
| *btitruk shughlak wa btuhrub* | Skip your work and sneak away |

17

| | |
|---|---|
| *wa ʿal kanteen bi truh tunsub* | To the Canteen with con tricks to play |
| *wallah la huttak fi charge* | By God, I will detain you |
| *wa amnaʿak roht el-kanteen* | And keep you away from the Canteen" |
| | |
| *wa shway jayyini el-captain* | Soon after, the Captain appeared |
| *wa bil-inglizi ʿam bi-rattain* | Bellowing in English |
| *Alli: "Do you speak English?"* | "Do you speak English?" he said |
| *Illtilu: "ba-rattil tarteel"* | "I can say a few things" |
| *Alli: "Where have you been?"* | "Where have been?" |
| *Illtilu: "Ya sidi, fi el-kanteen"* | "Sir, in the Canteen" |
| *Alli: "ʿalayk jiza yomain"* | "Your punishment's two days' pay" |
| *Illtilu: "fida ʿuyun Tsipora!"* | "A small price for gazing upon Tsipora!" |

*I do not remember* ever hearing my father sing this blues-y ditty, but the words and the tune are hard-wired into my brain. Total recall. When I sing it, they never hesitate or change. With my mind's eye, I can see young Arab men belting it out as they walk the night streets of Haifa during the last three years of Palestine's life. The years between the end of World War II and the Nakba of 1948. The years just before the English sergeant set sail for home, the canteens closed, and the proud and cocky young men themselves were killed or exiled, and their generation erased from history.

Erased, but not completely forgotten. How this ditty was im-planted in my brain and why this image comes to my mind, I do not know. I was born after Palestine and nothing—nothing I am consciously aware of, in any case—triggers this memory: no place, time, feeling, smell, sight, thought or any other association or context. The ditty is a perfectly pristine memory that is… well… not so memory-like. It must be a miracle memory: a memory of immaculate birth. No sex, no corporeal father, not even a mother screaming in agony as she gives birth in a cave upon a pile of hay.

*I do not remember* when I started to remember the ditty. But I am sure that I sang it many times before I was aware of it as a special memory. It is as if the ditty recalled me and not me it. And the funny

18

thing is that the words, as they bounce off my vocal chords, lilt to the accent of the rambunctious Mahatat al-Karmel neighborhood, a dense grove of lower middle class houses and small apartment buildings, sprawled between the English Cemetery and the Haifa Port, where the house my father was born in still stands. This accent—perfected by stonemasons, barbers, porters and chauffeurs, and slung around with gusto in kitchens and living rooms—no longer exists, and I, otherwise, cannot reproduce it. Obviously, the ditty—ensconced in my mind long before I became self aware—just sat there, patiently, waiting for me to grow up so I could conjure memory's box and open it.

*The song as a key to life* with a small "l": gritty, reckless, mean, generous, embarrassing, sexy, funny, transgressive and poignant life. A life of desires, heartaches, friendships, betrayals and bitter disappointments. A life whose textures cannot be captured by cardboard national narratives with their standard complements of heroes and villains.

*The song as a key to understanding* my father. That must have been the unconscious thought that suddenly compelled me to write it down on two small and shockingly flimsy pieces of paper. You know, the kind that starts to yellow as soon as it is exposed to air. Paper so thin that even the shyest ray of sun can make it shrivel, blacken and burn. I say "unconscious" because I then imagined I wrote it down for the same reason others record their memories: the fear of forgetting. I realize now that the opposite is true. I must have secretly hoped that the act of writing would transform it into a mortal memory: a memory that is born, lives and then dies. A normal memory that can be cited, shelved, then forgotten and forever lost, like an archive swept away in a mid-winter flood. I must have hoped that by writing down the ditty I would control and define it instead of it controlling and defining me. Writing as conquest. Writing as a crucifixion of the past. Writing as liberation.

*Freedom at last?* Hardly. *I do not remember* the act of writing the ditty. I do not even know at what age or where I was when I wrote it down. The two scraps of paper are proof that I did. The handwriting, shamefully messy and uncertain, is mine. Perhaps my brain moved faster than my agitated hands. That was my first thought as I stared at the clumsy script on brittle paper that miraculously survived for decades. But, not long after, I realized there is a more compelling explanation for the unruly scratches of ink: I must have jotted down the ditty sometime after the act of writing in Arabic had become unfamiliar to me and before it became familiar again. That would place this event somewhere in the middle of that purgatorial moment between leaving Lebanon (where my father had ended up as a refugee) at puberty and returning to it for the first time at the age of twenty-three. I spent that decade actively forgetting, then reclaiming the old world; and reluctantly embracing, then mastering the new one—all the while with nary a chance to speak or write in Arabic with anyone, as I left home not long after arriving in the United States. My previous life evaporated, suddenly and completely; and my new life, strange and unfamiliar, hurtled onwards without anchors or rest stops. Writing down the ditty must have marked the moment I became an adult, or at least the moment I (naively) thought that I could be in charge of my own life.

Yes, that must be it. After all, *this is a young man's ditty.* Its verses mock arrogant colonial masters and bourgeois sensibilities as they chase the pleasures of life with no thought of tomorrow. The words, intoxicated and defiant, run like hot blood in the veins of recently furloughed soldiers, and there is no resisting the desire to look through the billows of cigarette smoke into the eyes of Tsipora, the Jewish canteen girl.

*Nation? Destiny? Maybe.* But not tonight. Nothing like living through a world war for curing one of illusions about a brave new world. This is a ditty for boys who became men before their time and for men for whom manhood was the only game in town. Men who ran away from oppressive, hot-tempered fathers and drank from the tin cups of life as soldiers, merchant marines, service workers in military camps, couriers, smugglers, drivers. Teenage boys trained by whistles and barking dogs, who marched through Gaza and the Sinai to Egypt in long straight lines. Men who ran the supply lines across the deserts of North Africa, chased by bullets and shrapnel. Men who crossed the blue waters of the Mediterranean and learned a few Italian words as they pulled hard on their cigarettes under the shade of a hillside tree.

This is a ditty for men with loud voices and sarcastic smiles. Men armed with beer bottles and unfiltered Lucky Strikes. Men for whom paradise is octopus ink stew or a big bowl of small snails fed a diet of lettuce, starved, then boiled in big pots of water laced with aromatic spices. This is a ditty for fit and supremely confident young men in waist-high pants held in place by broad military-issue green canvas belts with big heavy metal buckles. Belts that sing like a whip when pulled out at lightning speed, snapped in the air, and brought down with explosive force on the nearest stationary object: a table, a wall, a bed. Men who level the world with the power of their swish, crackle and pop and who honor their word with stubborn pride. Men who survived and gave their all so others may as well. Men destined to die embittered and before their time.

The night streets of Haifa are silent. Afraid. They know not who owns them.

"Thank you very much, indeed... Beirut!" Why is that phrase also parked in my mind since the time before memories? What does it mean? And why is Beirut—where the people of Haifa found refuge from the barrels of gunpowder rolling down the Carmel hill—always added at the end of the phrase after a short pause? I do not know and I do not know if I will ever know. It is a Miracle Memory. A memory after Palestine.

21

# SHARIF S. ELMUSA

## Portable Absence:
## My Camp Re-membered

The weather there is temperate,
soil terra rosa.
The shepherds on the hills
have all but disappeared.
Winter sends modest rains,
animates the hardened earth:
red poppies swaying in the breeze,
little spokesmen of beauty;
cotton flowers, purple,
the sting of their thorns
final.

Not long after I arrived at Boston's Logan
Airport on July 1, 1971, I realized the magnitude of what I had left
behind—the landscape, family, friends, food, culture, words—my
constituents and extensions. I understood it was not a break that
could be welded, but rather a chemical reaction that could not be
reversed. I felt like "a capsule of the mind, a capsule in the wind,"
to paraphrase the poet Emily Dickinson.

Why did I leave? Because of the many maps I drew in school?
Or the sexual repression? Or the terror I felt at the drowning

22

of my cousins and playmates in the Jordan river when we were still adolescents? Or the bruises of the spirit inflicted by the defeats of Palestinians and other Arabs? Or simply to leave? Was I reenacting or running away from my parents' experience? Their escape, with more than three-quarters of a million Palestinians from their villages, was forced. Mine was voluntary and, instead of to a refugee camp, to the United States.

It wasn't the money. My civil engineering degree from the then prestigious Cairo University could have taken me to an oil-producing Gulf state and possibly made me well-off, like some cousins and friends. I jettisoned the engineering profession after a few years with a consulting firm in Boston.

> ...the demon that lures trains
> to derail, fires to rage,
> couples to sleep in discord,
> began to whisper his disquieting music,
> innuendos against blueprinted
> happiness...

> Look, beyond the walls
> there is a dim star, held by gravity,
> as you are by words.
> Trust yourself.

> He whispered until,
> one heedless day, I fled,
> fearing the known.

I cannot in this space say much about all the many creatures I have become—father, poet, scholar, university professor, political activist, airport regular—a backpack of contradictions. Instead, I will reflect on my refugee camp—Al-Nuwayma in Jericho, still in historic Palestine and yet across a new border from my parents' home on the coast—and the quandaries of exile and unrequited homesickness. Although living in a camp is the quintessential Palestinian experience, both actual and symbolic, relatively little has been written about it firsthand. I employ a combination of prose and poetry, most of the latter mine, some of it published and some in manuscript. Combining prose and poetry belongs to a long tradition of writing in Arabic that has since yielded to the uniform of Modernism.

Perhaps poetry is a form of exile or the two inter-act, like two medications, and amplify each other's action. Perhaps a poem is the silence in which the stranger wraps himself to pre-serve memory, to resist the gravity of the new abode. The capsule in the wind gains in density and rests for a moment, though only through the power of an unruly pen. Reading and writing poetry became my means to remember, to maintain awareness of myself as a person with a singular biography and subjectivity, to explore my estrangement.

But to write in English, and not in Arabic? A satisfactory answer may not be possible to this perennial question that all those who write in their non-native tongue ask themselves and are queried about by others. It may be a false question of modernity; nonetheless, it seems unavoidable. Whatever the reason, the decision to write in the non-native language is made neither by cold calculation nor with advance knowledge of the outcome. I did not think I had betrayed Arabic because, with hundreds of millions of speakers and countless writers and poets, that language is not a threatened species. In a sense, a new language is a home that is not a home.

Like the figure that C P Cavafy exhorts to, "Pour your Egyptian feelings into the Greek you use," I began to pour my Palestinian feelings into the English I penned. I had to mother my tongue and work harder than the language's own offspring. Perhaps all I could do was to "subtitle" myself. Writing in English brought me into a more intimate relationship with American culture and, at the same time, heightened my sense of exile. It relieved me of the burden of being a spokesman for the nation—perhaps an unavoidable tendency among Palestinian poets, at least in the early phases of their careers. And it guaranteed a wounding obscurity, a blessing and a curse for a poet.

Still, as someone from a family with more branches than a fig tree and one who has lived the experience of expulsion and camp dwelling, my poems bear the imprint of this milieu. Nor am I alone in my exile; I am in the company of many writers, poets, friends and others, dead and alive, who guide me and offer succour along the road.

> I once thought my poems revealed more
> about others and the world than about myself
> because I had repressed some traumatic memory.

> But now that Freud is dead, I feel free
> to say the reason is more mundane.

> I hail from a large family,
> with more branches than a fig tree.

Britain sends expats to other lands, India immigrants, and Palestine exiles. An expat is a "global" who has the luxury of maintaining a detached, if not humorous, distance from the affairs of the host country, exhibiting sympathy, disgust, arrogance, humility (rarely), likes and dislikes—all with an easy air. He will most likely go back (perhaps changed) to where he started from. In the myth and history of the journey, the expat is like the Arab-Muslim fourteenth century traveler, Ibn Battuta, who ventured as far as India and China secure in the knowledge that he could go back to Tangier. The immigrant, by contrast, wants to belong to, be accepted by, and have claims on the adopted shore. Without discounting the ambivalence and pain of the immigrant, either in coping with his novel circumstances or in longing for origins, he at least knows where he will prosper or fail, where he will retire and be buried.

A Palestinian exile lingers in a state of suspense, floats, lighter than the new social liquid, does not fuse. "In order to retain ownership over my distant sky/I must not own even my very skin," wrote Mahmoud Darwish.

While teaching in Doha recently, I must have felt such a need for renunciation:

> I can only go inside myself
> into the maze of the hippocampus
> which is like going inside a pyramid
> and finding the robbers had carted away
> the belongings.
> What will I shed this round
> to complete my portable absence?

No heroism intended, just an indication that a price must be paid. Even if I wanted to fuse into the United States, I would have fallen into all kinds of traps—imitation, insincerity and inability to be moved by sentiments that stir the natives as, for example, when they rise to sing the national anthem. I am not one to begrudge others their self-identification, but I would feel completely fake to say, as some immigrants do, "When *we* went into Afghanistan" (or Iraq or Panama or wherever), and talk about the people there as "them" and about themselves as "us." America is a land of opportunity, not of every opportunity.

I have been awed by its natural, sublime beauty and I admire the people's ingenuity and industry, their unassuming hospitality, and informality in dress and manner—their true stereotypes. I have no fondness for being the Other; and I am incapable, by my very constitution, of political and moral detachment from my environment. Most important, I am now bound to it by family: my wife, Judith Tucker, hails from West Hartford, Connecticut; my two children, Karmah and Layth, were born and raised in Washington, DC; and I have siblings and cousins and their offspring scattered throughout North America—their headcount may rival that of their counterparts in Jordan, where my natal family ended up after the 1967 Arab–Israeli war. Rather, my resistance to fusion is predicated on deep respect for other people's cultures and traditions; it takes several generations to belong truly to a place:

> The guest, my mother taught us, sits lightly
> on the outermost seat.

Odysseus—not Ibn Battuta or Abraham's journey towards a "promised land"—is the figure of homesickness and return in Palestinian writing, although it is a fraught comparison. Where is my Ithaca? Is it where I began? This is the common-sense idea of home. The refugee camp, however, was by definition not a home—it was a temporary transit station, even if my childhood there, despite the lack of modern technological comforts, was largely a happy one, filled with play and the warmth of family and friends, and was a "looking-forward." No one had any desire to stay in the camp or acknowledged it as his or her home.

On the wall of the room in which I studied and slept, hung a frame with a line from a poem by a high school teacher from Jerusalem, Adli Arafat, which my sisters had embroidered in white, black, red and green—the colors of the Palestinian flag—with Palestine as the title: "However long time keeps her and me apart/after the bitter separation we will be close." Although not a great verse, it did express a common sentiment.

Home was Palestine, the opposite of the camp, and the future was going to be the reverse of the here-and-now. It all depended on a news bulletin, a war, an uprising, a peace conference. It was, and continues to be, a state of enduring expectation, never mind that the Palestinians have always ended up on the losing side of each event.

"There, on the mountain top/our houses stood," said the young Jordanian poet, Rifaat Al-Salibi, shortly after the 1948 Nakba, identifying completely with the Palestinian refugees, in a poem I memorized at school. For me, it was there, in the village of my birth, Al-Abbasiyya, next to the city of Lyd—

far enough from the sea
not to spawn sailors,
close enough to have horizon.
The highway made a small gesture
to its modest homes.

My parents tilled the red earth,
their young backs stooped over it,
made it articulate with oranges and grapes.

Memories flash in unexpected ways, shake me into
acknowledging them, and let me go. The refugee camp ambushes
me anywhere, any moment.

Marvelling today at the Safeway's abundance
of tuna fish cans,
I remember my friend Hussein.
He was the genius of the school.
He breathed in history, grammar, math
as easily as he breathed the dust of the camp.

Or:

The streets were laid out in a grid,
as in New York,
but without the dignity of names
or asphalt.

As if I visited that great city to rediscover the camp. I realized
how the camp was a modern contraption: a grid; a main street for
shops and public facilities, including a health clinic, schools and a
police station, all alongside two roads on the south and west sides.
The refugee camps and New York City—the place where our camps,
these putatively temporary residences, were concocted by United
Nations personnel—now became inseparable, present memory, two
distant objects juxtaposed without surrealist intention. Which was
the mirror of the other, the camp or New York City?

In the mid-Seventies, on a trip that took me to New Mexico, I visited the Native American "reservation," Taos Pueblo. The reservation's mud houses, wooden girders protruding from the ceilings, the streets muddied by rainwater—all evoked instantaneously the landscape of Al-Nuwayma, my camp. Taos Pueblo's houses were abutted by a green mountain; the high hills overlooking our camp, which we called mountains, were barren, except for a sprinkle of green in the spring. The population of Al-Nuwayma was around five thousand, or about five times that of the reservation. In Taos and in Santa Fe, I "saw" pottery for the first time. The desert colors and geometric designs were stunningly beautiful, embodied a heritage, and shone with a will to life. I still have a teapot from that visit sitting on a bookshelf in the living room. The Native Americans placed their colors on their clothes and jewelry and pottery; the Palestinian camps were colorless, except for the women's embroidered dresses and the profusely-colored marbles of which I was an avid player and which—in addition to the night sky with its villages of stars, mysterious milky ways, and arresting moons—perhaps made me thirst for art and made me want to create beauty in the way I could, with words.

I should have engaged the residents about their history and mine, but I couldn't be certain if such a move would be well-received, since I was a tourist like any other, part of the people who took over their land, a settler like those I do not want to see arriving in Palestine. Thanks to the poet Edgar Silex, the Palestinian/Native American connection has been made in a most ironic, poignant manner. His *Chief Nanay Appears in the Holy Land* evokes the Apache, Nanay, who was wounded fourteen different times defending his land, in the figure of a Gaza man wounded, and then killed, by Israeli gunners—and also brings forth the terrible irony of the Apache helicopter that bombarded the Gazan's family house after his death.

It is a political oxymoron, even if a privilege, to be from a tiny, colonized country struggling to rid itself of Israeli domination and, at the same time, to be a citizen of an empire that is the principal keeper of Israel. What/how to feel when I see President Barack Obama posing for a photo op with a vassal, or someone who made himself into one, like Mahmoud Abbas, the President of the Palestinian Authority? How to vote in the elections when nearly all the candidates compete to demonstrate not only their support for Israel, but also their love of it? I voted twice, once for Jesse Jackson and the second time for Ralph Nader, only partly because of their positions on Palestine—desperate gestures, no doubt. Still, it would seem that the only way to reconcile my being a Palestinian and an American citizen is to fit my consciousness on a political procrustean bed.

The experience of exile is not the same everywhere. My residency since I left the camp alternated between Arab countries and the United States. The shift in place itself is confusing even for me and I cannot tell my story in a clean, continuous narrative. Studying in Cairo in 1967, I lived the defeat of the Arab armies in June that year and the occupation of the West Bank by Israel. In the aftermath, Israel denied me, as it did hundreds of thousands of other Palestinians, the right to go back not only to the territory that became Israel in 1948, it barred us in a similar fashion from the West Bank and my camp, Al-Nuwayma. I became, as a consequence, a "displaced person," in the UN's legal lexicon, a refugee from a refugee camp.

Cairo could not have been more different when I returned in 1999 to teach at the American University of Cairo. In the 1960s, during Gamal Abd Al-Nasser's presidency, it was the "beating heart" of Arab nationalism, the center of Arab high culture, a promoter of social equity, a stalwart advocate of the Palestinian "cause," and a hub of African liberation and the nonaligned movements. All that was reversed with the isolationist, neoliberal turn in Egyptian political and economic life under Presidents Anwar Sadat and Hosni Mubarak. Official Egypt struck a separate peace deal with Israel in 1979; Cairo lost its status as the moral/political core of the Arab region; a class of nouveau riche grabbed most of the country's wealth as the mass of the poor swelled; corruption and distrust permeated the remotest interstices of government and society; repression of political life by the security apparatus was the same as it was under Nasser, if not worse; and individual Egyptians saw their prestige diminish outside Egypt.

> We don't have bicycle lanes marked
> by wine-red paint. Everyday we stage
> the grand opera, How things don't work.
> Perfection is as rare as rainfall or smallpox…

> If the whistle of the rusty freight train
> grates your ear, take it for what it is:
> a politician's rhetoric
> independent of the freight.

The overthrow of the Mubarak regime by the January 25 Revolution in 2011 was overdue, if unanticipated. What will the scent of the "new air," as Egyptians call the new order, be like eventually? Will Palestine, for a change, profit from it?

Cairo, like all cities, cannot be grasped or reduced to some essence. If you make a generalization about it at night, the bright morning sunlight is likely to wash it away. The city continually buffets the senses like the ocean's waves, with both coolness and salt, except that the assault is waged by cars and humans, their bodies and sounds and smells and their chaotic movement, visible and invisible, present and past:

> Life is down to its simplest expressions,
> at last.
> It takes all the never-minds,
> the jasmine of humor,
> for the senses to mend.

Cairo's maddening imperfections can be a paradise for the imagination; its terrible means of transportation a means of transport.

Cairenes reminded me, without intending to, not to believe my own propaganda about not fusing. In more than one casual encounter, the interlocutor would say to me, "You must have been living abroad," as if I wore the mark of a mobile Cain on my forehead. It might have been the way I did not roll my "r," my demeanor, my hesitations or who knows what, that gave me away. A doorman who lived, like so many others of his ilk, in a damp room in the country that is home to the sun god Ra, asked me once to bring him Bengay for his arthritis, and added, "Mr. Jack used to." The most hilarious was a taxi driver whose head was undoubtedly loaded with hashish. He addressed me as "Mistur," which, with the spread of the English language, underclass Egyptians used to refer to a foreigner, instead of the old Turkish *khawaga*. I tried to persuade him I was not a Mistur, and that pants and a shirt did not make me one. I said if I were a Mistur, he also had to be one. He stared at me, turned his face, and said, in a grave voice, "Look at me: do I look like a Mistur?" The only thing I could do was to laugh out loud.

> When we meet those who stayed
> themselves, we put on airs
> and mock their simple fins
> and they, they stare at us
> with slanted eyes:
> "How odd these amphibians,
> what shall we do about them?"

Almost every modern metropolis has shanty towns, barrios or '*ash-waiyyat*, "the-at-random," as they call them in Cairo those often illegal habitations of rural immigrants and the urban poor. Their residents are not exactly refugees, but they too dream of moving elsewhere to better-heeled neighborhoods. In Cairo, and specifically on the metro and in downtown squares and streets, my childhood peers haunted me. I could see them in the young Egyptian boys who crowded the trains which I took almost daily to the campus, located until a couple of years ago in the heart of Cairo, in the now legendary Tahrir Square.

The man who goes everyday
to the same work place,
on the same narrow tracks,
is he happy or sad?

It is not love of misery or poverty, nor just a cultivated intellectual stance that prompted me to listen to and write about them,
but rather a felt affinity, the spontaneous poetry in their words,
the wry humor, like that of my father and mother—we "re-vision"
what digs most deeply in our consciousness, what amplifies and is
amplified by memory.

On a furnace-hot train one summer afternoon:

A man, wiping the sweat off his face, wonders
aloud,
"Why don't they turn on the fans?"
Another, quick, used to the absurd,
"They turn them off in summer
to turn them on in winter."

Why did I write without much hesitation about everyday Egypt
and even its ancient gods and symbols, but didn't find or didn't try
to find a way to write about America? Because I could feel or think
like the Egyptians or read their minds, but couldn't do the same
with Americans?

I have been back in Palestine fairly regularly on
tourist visas granted, after much harassment in and out, by Israeli
personnel at the land ports between Jordan and the West Bank or at
Ben Gurion Airport, which stretches out on part of the land of my
village. I have lived during these trips for varying lengths of time
in Gaza, Jerusalem, Nablus and Ramallah—two cities that, when I
was at school, my family and I also summered in, to escape Jericho's
oppressive heat—and I have been to see the camp and the village
on more than one occasion.

The longest stay was in Jerusalem in 1994–95, a year after the Oslo agreement, about which I had severe misgivings. It quickly became clear that Israel was going to persist in its policy of taking over West Bank land and of keeping the Palestinian population under control. Nonetheless, I thought Palestinians should try to steer the agreement to their advantage and seize whatever opportunities it might open up to improve their position. I wanted to help in this endeavor however I could, like many others who trickled in for the same purpose.

My family and I did not go to see the camp until March 1994. We went together with our friends, Mary McKone and Fateh Azzam, and their two children. We had met in Boston and worked together with the Committee of Palestinians in New England, trying to reach out to the American public. Now we were all reunited in Ramallah.

I had been told by relatives and had read in an article in 1985 in *Filastin Al-Thawra*, the PLO's mouthpiece, that the camp had been bulldozed in mid-July of the previous year, followed a year later by the two other camps around Jericho, Aqbat Jabr and Ayn Al-Sultan. (The three camps were built near the ancient town thanks to the presence of several water springs.) The camp's mud houses had disintegrated, the Israeli army used it as training ground, and mosquitoes buzzed about, said the article. Nonetheless, I still wanted to see it for myself and to show the camp to my kids. My parents had taken me back to our village through their stories until I visited it many years later and found it transformed. I had done the same with my children about the camp, and now we were going to see its ruins.

The refugee camp is looked upon with pity by Palestinians themselves. No one likes refugees and no one wants to be or to be called one. I was not surprised when the residents of New Orleans, who fled after hurricane Katrina devastated the city, objected with vehemence to be referred to as refugees. The camp-dwellers have borne the brunt of the immense sacrifices that Palestinians as a whole have paid on the altar of the "cause," but have not been, and are not likely to be, rewarded with the commensurate regard. Two

34

of the most memorable instances are the massacres of the Sabra and Shatila camps and the devastation of the Jenin camp. In Sabra and Shatila in Beirut, right wing Christian militias murdered about three thousand people, abetted by the Israeli army during its invasion of Lebanon in 1982. They were hurled into mass graves,

> the earth was so dumbfounded
> it could not cry: "Enough"

The Jenin camp in the West Bank was partly destroyed when its residents decided, in 2002, to stand up to Israeli forces which had rolled into West Bank cities and towns to crush the Second Intifada. Mahmoud Darwish, whose chronicle of the journey of the Palestinian "soul" after 1967 is unequalled, wrote precious little about the camps. The camp, in this sense, is a zone of exile in the Palestinian mind. It takes a reservoir of inner freedom and self-confidence for those who stay, or even those who leave, to heal the laceration of living in that flawed quarter.

I did not want my kids to find themselves abruptly, without introduction, in the camp. They had to be prepared, I reasoned, and be spared the shock and perhaps the embarrassment of having their father come from such a humble place. So we stopped first at the sixth century Greek Orthodox monastery carved into the heart of the Mount of Temptation, where Jesus is said to have fasted for forty days and forty nights during Satan's temptation and uttered, "not by bread alone." The Mount cradled the town of Jericho below and overlooked the three camps—Aqbat Jabr to the south and Ayn Al-Sultan and Al-Nuwayma to the north, which were separated from each other by a dry-bed *wadi*. It was not hard to see our destination from the lookout at the monastery. "There it is," I said, pointing with my forefinger, "that cluster of tall trees, poplar trees, that's the border of the camp."

Afterwards, we descended the steep staircase which we had climbed to reach the monastery, then drove to Hisham's Palace on the southwestern rim of the camp. The palace was named after

Hisham Ibn Abd Al-Malik, the eighth century Omayyad caliph during whose reign the Arab-Muslim empire extended from the Pyrenees to India. The palace facing the camp: a more poignant image of the contrast between the state of the Arabs then and now could not have been dreamed up by the wildest poet. It was a disorienting moment for me to act like a tourist; I could not escape the befuddled gaze of the child I myself was who had walked by the palace almost daily.

Did I want to go into the camp and disturb that child? What would he think of my picture being taken with blond kids and sun-glassed women? Would he treat me with curiosity and ambivalence the way he had treated the tourists of his time? Only occasionally did a young man or woman visitor stray into the camp; then, he and his friends would invite the visitor for tea and coffee and even meals, and query their guest about his or her country, explaining in fragmented school English the "Question of Palestine," small, dusty-faced and barely-shod Edward Saids.

I told myself the critical child should understand, and might recognize himself in my children: in my daughter's broad lips, son's strong chin, the curly hair and argumentativeness of both. He might not find even their blue eyes remarkable: his mother and some of his siblings were blue-eyed.

We found, as anticipated, that the camp had been leveled and the site covered with rubble. No house was spared. When the German poet Rainer Maria Rilke remembered his childhood abode, he said he felt it was broken into pieces inside him; the inward shattering of the self produced the outward breaking of the house. In my case, the feeling of being shattered moved in the opposite direction.

The only structures that were not demolished were the property of UNRWA, the United Nations agency responsible for Palestinian refugees. One of these was my middle school. Its buildings of concrete and stone had withstood the workings of time, except that the doors and windows were boarded up with cinder blocks, the faucets removed from the water tank where we used to

36

drink, and the wooden doors from the row of Turkish toilets. The weathered and faded walls were covered with nationalist graffiti, including demands for the freedom of Palestinian prisoners in Israeli jails. The kids seemed delighted to be in the school and it was an oddly exhilarating encounter, not without a touch of the absurd. I showed my company the classrooms and the administration offices, the yard where we lined up in the morning, the volleyball field, and other facilities. While the adults were talking the children seemed to have disappeared. I went looking for them and, oops, found the four of them, each squatting on a toilet pretending to poop, and we all burst out laughing. One of the classrooms' concrete board-ups had been breached, and the kids bent their backs and slipped in through the narrow hole. They were thrilled when they emerged, saying they had found a blackboard and chalk and scribbled their names on the board. Layth said he really liked entering a classroom through a hole and asked, "Dad, did you do this everyday?"

Having had the kids visit my school, run where I ran, squat on the same toilet, and scribble on the same board, I felt my life was complete.

In the beginning the Eraser razed the village.

He let the villagers be frightened into fleeing their
houses and their fields,
and He saw that they had fled,
and He heard the ghosts talking
strange talk in the empty houses,
and He let the houses be rubble, without form,
and let the stray animals roam the site,
and He saw that the sight was an unnecessary
reminder,

...and He saw all that He unmade and,
O wow, was it good and, on the sixth day, He took
a break.

Waking up on the seventh day,
He saw that the refugees had multiplied
and become fabulists, conjuring forest fires.

I did not need the houses in the camp to be standing to see them; after the initial disbelief, the mouse of memory placed them back precisely in their former order, as in a computer game. I stood at the spot that was the beginning of our street and pointed out where the Elmusas' houses were. The neighbors were from nearby villages—al-Naani, Salama, Aqir and Ajjur. At the far end of the street was the single-room house of an old woman from a tribe in Bir Al-Saba' (Beersheba). She wore all the Bedouin accoutrement: the silver ring in the pierced nose, the crown with old silver coins and colorful beads, the tattoos on her cheeks and chin (which later made the body piercings of the young in the West appear more amusing than original). It was as if someone had taken the former villagers and shuffled them and rearranged their residences, rendering the camp a little Palestine, a melting pot of diverse accents, dresses and temperaments. No wonder Palestinian nationalism and resistance burgeoned in the refugee enclaves.

Whatever we learned of our history and villages, however, was from the telling of the older people who had lived there—there was nothing about them in the school curriculum. I pictured the villages to be standing as they were described; only years later did I realize they were mostly obliterated by Israel to prevent our return.

As luck would have it, I "returned" more than once. In the late 1980s, I joined a team of Palestinian scholars to produce an encyclopedia-style volume documenting the geography, history and current state of all the villages that were depopulated during 1947–48. I was immersed in the life of these villages for two years—writing their histories, village by razed village.

As I wrote, I felt I was composing individual elegies of villages that had been built to last. A village existed, sometimes from prehistory, with continuous Arab/Muslim presence for fifteen hundred years or so, suffered partial or total (mostly total) physical excision at the hands of the Israelis, and the sites of many such villages were now covered by forests. Our team identified four hundred and eighteen villages of various sizes spread throughout the area that became Israel in 1948—most of which were razed.[1]

Beyond the physical erasure, I could not believe, although was not surprised by, how these villages had also been concealed by a "forest of text." Israeli histories and encyclopedias absented them, truncated their biographies, presented selective information, and employed convoluted terminology. Where Jewish settlements had been built over the sites, the names were changed or modified into a Hebrew equivalent. One word that often occurred in Israeli sources to describe a former village was "abandoned," with no cause offered. Only recently have a new crop of Israeli historians and novelists begun to clear that forest and expose the misdeeds of their forbears.

Before working on the project, I made two abortive visits to my village, Al-Abbasiyya (now Yehud). The first time was in 1976 when I rented a taxi from Ramallah driven by a man who grew up in the village. At the entrance, an elderly guard stopped us to check our IDs and ask why we were there. I told him I had been born in the village and wanted to see it. He was about to let us in when a bunch of young men emerged from a pool hall and yelled at us in Hebrew. We were not welcome. So the driver sped through the streets and pointed to a few extant Palestinian houses and the mosque.

I went back again in the summer of 1986 or 1987—I can't recall exactly—with my wife and our friends, Mary and Fateh. As we prepared to set off from Jerusalem in their car, there was news of an Israeli teacher killed by a Palestinian in the area of Tulkarem, and the atmosphere grew tense. We decided to go anyway. But we didn't feel safe being in the village once we got there. We sat at a sidewalk café and ordered tea with mint, which the waiter called by its Arabic, *naanaa*. We drank the tea quickly, wondering if it was safe. Then we took a quick tour and I could see what were probably the old café,

Arab houses and the mosque, in a state of disrepair. Once more, a furtive, unsatisfying visit—a running-into, not a reunion with, my birthplace. I felt as if I were an adopted son and went back to my biological parents and they rejected me. I could only imagine the enormity of despair that my parents and the hundreds of thousands of others felt at being uprooted; "uprooted" is still an apt word to describe that event, especially if the tree is old and its roots have spread profusely in the earth, and you can feel the tremendous force that pulled them out and listen to the sound of them tearing.

My friend, Fateh, braved hauling the ashes of his father, who had died in Florida, through Israeli airport security and executed his will and buried the urn in Nazareth, his birthplace. Ibrahim Abu Lughod, a prominent Palestinian–American political scientist, was also buried by stealth in Jaffa, where he was born. Few diaspora Palestinians, however, have the "luxury" of being buried in Palestine. Others have gone to perform what might be called "rituals of return" before the end of their lives. Aziz Shihab, the father of the poet Naomi Shihab Nye, went back to his village, surveyed the fields, gazed at the earth, moistened the soil with his tears, said adieu, and left to die in Texas. The question of the place of burial is an exile's nightmare. Perhaps, as the Hungarian poet Attila Jüzsef said, home is where people can read your name correctly on the tombstone. The Israeli residents of my birthplace would not even wish to read my name, although they could probably pronounce it better than people in Washington DC.

Reflecting on the park of his childhood, Antoine de Saint-Exupéry wrote in *Wind, Sand, and Stars:* "What do we learn except that in this infinity we shall never set foot, and that it is into the game and not the park that we have lost the power to enter." I can enter neither the park nor the game. To recount my experience in the diaspora and faux returns is not, I hope, an exercise in nostalgia, although there is, unfortunately, much to be sentimental about. It is about the present and the future. For me, Palestine, like any other country, cannot be home if it does not welcome the Other. Palestine is a forward-looking Odyssean quest inclusive of the suitors; an ideal to search for, to despair, and even to be afraid of finding. Furies, gentle and monstrous, still lie ahead and keep me in a frame of mind akin to the blues—feeling homesick when you know you don't have a home.

> Scores of fishing boats
> spread out
> of the meager port.
> In the depth of the night
> their kerosene lamps
> an oasis of lights,
> soft, yellow—
> a beauty
> hard to conquer
> or resist.
>
> The fishermen doze off,
> and row again.

**Note**

1 Walid Khalidi et al., *All That Remains: The Palestinian Villages Occupied and Depopulated by Israel in 1948* (Beirut and Washington DC: Institute for Palestine Studies, 1992).

# LILA ABU-LUGHOD

## Pushing at the Door:
## My Father's Political Education,
## and Mine

"Say goodbye." This is what the doctor said softly to us in the middle of the night. We had telephoned him in panic and he had come out in the dark to his friend's apartment, despite the eerie emptiness of Ramallah's streets in the midst of the Second Intifada. He had followed the stages of our father's illness from the first crisis in February. Mercifully, he had some morphine with him, which stopped the shuddering pain. My sister and I awakened our aunt. "Come say goodbye," I whispered. Shocked, she ran into her brother's room. She'd been praying hard for him. She felt betrayed.

It was May 23, 2001. As dawn lightened the sky, people began to arrive, so many of them who had shared the nine years of my father's rich new second life in Palestine. My father, Ibrahim Abu-Lughod, had moved back in 1992, after more than forty years of exile, most of it spent in the United States. After struggling to get a college education, then going to graduate school, he'd led a busy life as a scholar and professor of political science, teaching at Smith College, McGill University and then Northwestern, with interludes on educational projects in the Arab world. He had raised a family with my mother, Janet, a sociologist and urban planner, who came to do research in the Arab world through him but whose commitments to justice were her own. His life had revolved around Palestine and he had instilled in us, his children, a sense of our Palestinianness despite

43

our American lives and his own vivid participation in everything from academic politics (what he referred to as "village politics") to an intense and stormy marriage, suburban lawn-mowing, and the challenges of shepherding teenagers into adulthood in the US.

Ever since he'd felt the stinging humiliation of what he perceived as Americans' glee over Israel's defeat of the Arabs in 1967, he had thrown himself into public speaking and organizing in the US about Middle East issues—he wanted to combat the deep hostility and ignorance he found all around him. He was heckled. He was attacked. Fortunately, his university protected him under the banner of academic freedom, but also because he was such an engaging teacher and colleague. Eventually he focused his energies on the Palestine question. He talked and wrote about the historical injustice of Palestinian dispossession; he dreamed of liberation. He also spoke pragmatically about politics and worked to establish Arab-American intellectual institutions as alternatives to the mainstream. At the back of his closet in Ramallah we were to find a small leather suitcase stuffed with yellowed newspaper clippings documenting his appearances at everything from a press conference at the US State Department to Arab community meetings in obscure middle-American towns. His international speaking had taken him from Ghana to Australia. A soft little kangaroo skin in his Ramallah apartment was the out-of-place memento of this last trip.

What had brought him to Ramallah was a medical crisis in 1990 that forced on him a sense of mortality. He told people he feared he might die before seeing Palestine again. He decided to return. First for a visit, then to live. But not in Jaffa, his birthplace—that was part of Israel now and he refused to submit himself to direct rule by those who had taken his country and city. (He did try to get a post office box there, just for the thrill of having a Jaffa address. He was refused.) He could not claim his birthright, which Israel does not recognize, even though any Russian or Ethiopian who claims Jewish roots (and even some who don't) can get housing and financial support from the state, and thousands of American Jewish teenagers get free holidays as their birthright. Instead, he moved to the Occupied West Bank, to Ramallah. His status: tourist. Although he came to take up a longstanding invitation to teach at Birzeit University, work permits are rarely given by the Israelis, so he used his American passport. He had to leave and re-enter the country every three months to renew this tourist visa.

Like many 1948 refugees, my father had no family left in Palestine. They had been scattered by the fighting of 1948 and the general expulsion. His world in Ramallah consisted of friends and colleagues, not relatives. It was they who came to his apartment when they heard the news that he was dying. These were all people who shared his commitment to Palestinians and to building Palestinian institutions. They appreciated his optimism in the face of grim realities. He had lightened up a tense world of curfews, insecurity and humiliation with his affection and humor.

From the moment he arrived, he insisted on traveling around *his* Palestine, refusing to recognize the borders of the Green Line that marks off what was taken in 1948 from what was occupied in 1967. He made friends in Haifa and 'Akka and Nazareth. He made a special point of going regularly to Jaffa, taking anyone who had the right kind of travel documents to get through the Israeli checkpoints. He loved the defiant but embattled community that kept Jaffa alive. Most of all, he liked to swim in the sea that he had loved as a boy. He felt he was home.

Since his arrival in 1992, he had dedicated himself to one project after another that he saw as part of nation-building. Most of the people who arrived one by one at his apartment for the sad vigil were those with whom he had worked on these projects. First, his colleagues and friends from Birzeit University, the first Palestinian university, founded in 1972. There, he had sought to revive and contribute to academic life after years of closures. My father had described to a colleague what it was like to teach at Birzeit in the early 1990s when he first arrived:

I started teaching at a very exciting period. The Israelis were still in Ramallah. Every few days there was a curfew and I could see the tanks and the jeeps. It was an occupied country, no question about it. I saw people being arrested and beaten by the army on a daily basis. Ramallah would close around two o'clock... Because of this environment, it was impossible for the university to function as other universities do. Birzeit could be closed at a moment's notice after being surrounded by the army.[1]

Some of the other friends who arrived at my father's apartment as he lay dying had been part of the committed team he had assembled to design the first unified independent Palestinian national curriculum. For the past few years, my father's passion had been the planning of another major national institution: a Palestinian national museum. Not one that would focus on the Nakba like a Holocaust memorial that dwelt only on the tragedy of one historic moment of loss and devastation, but a museum that would, as he insisted, communicate the continuous existence of the Palestinians on the land, assert a living national history, and serve as a resource for historical research and archiving.

So many others were there in the Ramallah apartment: people who had worked with him, studied under him, or simply enjoyed the animated political discussions he always engaged in, accompanied by the good food he relished and often cooked himself. Mahmoud Darwish, Palestine's great poet, had come to visit nearly every day of my father's illness. In a few days he would eulogize his friend, complimenting his warmth, his pragmatism and his vision. "Like other great men with missions," he would say, "he did not write as much as he was actively involved in daily intellectual discussion, defending a hope besieged by powers that could only be defeated by optimism of the will."[2]

Many, especially the women, had waited until daylight before coming, fearful of the insecurity of the Second Intifada triggered in late 2000 by Ariel Sharon's provocative visit with soldiers to the Aqsa Mosque in Jerusalem. It was May 2001 now and the intermittent gunfire on the outskirts of Ramallah between the Israeli army and locals reminded us all that one never knew what was going to happen. Just a week earlier the Israelis had bombed a house across from the Grand Park Hotel, a small establishment only a few blocks away from my father's apartment. The explosion had set off the alarm on his oxygen machine and panicked him. "Quick, get in the corridor," he'd ordered my sisters and aunt. "That's what we did in Beirut when the Israelis bombed. It's the safest place."

In the stories my father told about the past, especially when he was spinning them for his younger political admirers, he presented a seamless myth of his political trajectory back to Palestine. His mother was a surprisingly strong presence in these stories. Two sets of interviews, one in Arabic and one in English, the first recorded in August 1982 while Beirut was under siege[3] and the second between 1999–2000, by Hisham Ahmed-Fararjeh in Ramallah, suggest that her inclusion in his own story of expulsion from Palestine and in the larger epic of the Palestinians' losses had a symbolic dimension. She was certainly a strong figure and herself a storyteller, like him. She was, my mother explained to me, his real link to what everyday life in pre-1948 Palestine had been like. But in his stories, she seems to stand for what they had all lost, and to justify his own politicization.

He was only eighteen years old when the fighting broke out in Jaffa in 1947—fighting that would, with the British departure, result in the Zionist forces seizing Jaffa, the cultural and economic capital of Arab Palestine, despite the fact that the UN Partition Plan that recommended the division of Palestine into Jewish and Arab parts had designated Jaffa as part of the Arab Palestinian state. When their neighborhood of Manshiyya—on the border with Tel Aviv—became too dangerous, they moved out to stay with an uncle. He lived in downtown Jaffa, in 'Ajami, over the gold market and near the "Palace" (the local municipality building), but after a Zionist paramilitary group set off an explosion in the Palace, killing sixty-nine people while my father was sitting in the Islamic Youth Club nearby, he was badly shaken and decided to move the family to another place.

He liked to tell the story of how he found a modern apartment as a temporary home—an apartment whose owners, like most of Jaffa's bourgeoisie with money and connections, had fled abroad in the early days of the fighting. This couple had allegedly gone on their honeymoon. What he most vividly remembered was his mother's response: "My whole family started cursing: 'What brought us to this house?!' It had a western-style toilet. And a shower! They wanted the ordinary familiar things. We told them, 'Let's thank God we found somewhere to live.' But there were more complaints: 'And on the third floor? How are we supposed to go up and down?'"

His mother, he said, didn't like the modern neighborhood and berated him for separating her from her friends. "She was upset. There were a million problems. There was no public bakery [most families in traditional neighborhoods made the dough at home but took the loaves to be baked in communal ovens]. We had to buy bread, but my mother refused. 'This is inedible!' She wasn't used to this kind of life."

As the fighting between the Zionist forces and the Palestinians intensified, with skirmishes between Jaffa and Tel Aviv getting worse, he and his eldest brother (both of whom by April were working with the hastily formed, disorganized, and barely-armed National Committee to Defend Jaffa) told the rest of the family they should leave the city. There was hardly any food and no end in sight to the fighting. He and his brother were finding it almost impossible to scour the city for food. Everyone had heard of the massacre and the rapes in Deir Yassin and they feared for their young sister, Raja. My father said to his interviewers in Beirut:

> My mother didn't want to leave, she was a fighter. But we told her, "No, you have to. You can go to Nablus, it's not far and we'll soon follow. Things are sure to calm down." (We were just leading her along.) So we brought them a truck and we put them in it... My brother was only

48

fifteen. There was no one who could take charge except my mother. We thought it would be a matter of a week or two. It never occurred to me that we would never return.

My father himself finally left in May on what was rumored to be the last boat out of Jaffa. As he described it, the shooting was all coming from the other side—there was hardly anyone left in Jaffa. His mother's experience symbolized all that was lost when they lost Palestine. My father told his interviewers in Beirut:

> I'll tell you something. I asked my mother many years later, maybe it was 1976. I said, "Ya Hajja, we've heard that they might be giving compensation. What do you think? Would you take compensation for what you lost?" She answered, "God damn them… How could you compensate me? I want to live with my community, they destroyed my community. What do I want with the money?" There were a few families from Jaffa who lived near her in Amman, this was why she wanted to stay there. She'd come and visit us all [her sons] but she refused to live anywhere else. There were three families, her friends, who had been with her in Jaffa—on the same street, in the same neighborhood. They stayed together, they would visit her, she'd visit them. And when she died, they were the same families that came together. For her, Jaffa and the whole country, meant this community.

My grandmother was also a recurring figure in the story of his political awakening which, as he told it in the late 1990s when he himself was approaching seventy, culminated in his finding his community as a Palestinian. This happened first in the politics of liberation and later in his return (*'awda*) to live, work and, as it turned out, to die on Palestinian soil. She appears in an early memory of going to his first demonstration in Jaffa. He thinks it was in 1936, around the time of the general strike to protest the British failure to halt Zionist colonization. He says the British called it a riot, as was typical of colonial politics. But he understood it now as an uprising, an intifada. He remembers taking his young brother on his shoulders.

It was a huge demonstration and I saw… the British army and British police mounted on horseback with big batons, beating the heads of our people. I saw blood streaming from the heads and was so scared by the sight that I kept saying to my younger brother, who was just an idiot, four years old: "Did you see that!! Did you see that?" I was trying to reassure myself but he was screaming, the poor thing, "Yes, yes, I see, I see."[4]

He recalls the chants: "'Down with British imperialism!' 'Down with the Balfour Declaration.' 'Down with Zionism!' It was all down with this and that." He jokes, "We never heard the word up!" The lesson for the present that he drew from his childhood story is that those who now accuse Palestinian mothers of sending their children out to throw stones in the intifada are absurd.

I remember that in my case nobody pushed me to go to the demonstration. I knew exactly that it was anti-British and anti-Zionist. There was no doubt at the age of seven who were the enemies of the Palestinians… The interesting thing is that when I came back from the demonstration after the British had succeeded in overcoming the uprising and beating the hell out of our people, arresting our people, injuring our people, my mother opened the door for me and began to scold me. She wasn't scolding me because I went to the demonstration, she was scolding me because I took my younger brother with me. "How dare you take your younger brother?" You see, he didn't understand anything. So, it was okay for me at the age of seven to go, *I* was old enough to understand. His commentary then turned to the present: The mothers understand what their children are doing. They cannot restrain them or imprison them at home because this is a national action for liberation.[5]

His life story of political activism oscillated between marvel at the absurdity of his own ignorance and pride in his efforts and transformation. As a high school student in the final days of the British Mandate, he was active in mobilizing students around the country. Sometimes he had to lie to his mother and tell her he was off studying. He talks about his disillusionment later, when it dawned on him in the months after they were all forced to flee Jaffa, that the Arab armies had no plans to take Palestine back. He talks of the humiliations he endured as a refugee in Jordan when his family finally settled there in 1949, Nablus not having turned out to be workable because of the huge influx of other refugees. Not only were they living crowded into one room, with no glass in the windows so that they either got wet in the rain or suffocated by stuffing the windows full of blankets, but they lost all the economic security they had had in Jaffa, as well as his dreams of future educa-tion. He had dreamed of being a lawyer; his grandfather had been a judge. The sudden loss of social standing was the worst. He said, "You are in a place where no one knows you."

Because Amman was inundated by hundreds of thousands of Palestinian refugees, the monarch was afraid that Jordan would be destabilized. The Jordanian police would round up the refugees and insult them. As he told his interviewers in Beirut, it pained my father to hear what they said:

> "All of you are pimps, sons of bitches. You sold your land to the Jews. All of you collaborated." And I don't know what else they said. We had never thought of ourselves as part of a mass; we had been living in Jaffa; we were from such and such family; our family's home was in such and such a place; and we were connected to these other people. And we were respectable... My father was respected, a nationalist. People knew us. We had dignity.

No more.

My father finally escaped to the United States in 1949, by boat, on borrowed money. My uncle tells me that he left just in the nick of time as the authorities came to the house looking for him soon after, having arrested some of his political friends. In the US he pur-sued his education while working menial jobs, like any immigrant. By 1954 he had married, had his first child (me), and was doing a PhD at Princeton.

Antagonism towards the Palestinians reappeared as a strong theme in his description of one of the most significant turning points in his political life: attending his first meeting of the Palestine National Council. On a visit to Egypt in August 1970, he met his friend, the noted Egyptian journalist, Mohammad Hassanein Heykal, at the Al-Ahram Center for Political and Strategic Studies. Heykal invited him to lunch in the cafeteria, mysteriously saying there were some people he might like to meet. To my father's utter surprise, it turned out to be Yasser Arafat, accompanied by some key figures in the recently formed PLO. He was stunned. "I was shy: My God! This was our leadership!" After some small talk, he says he summoned up the courage to ask a question. Looking straight at Arafat, who was wearing his dark glasses and *kuffiya*, he asked, "Mr. Arafat, what role do you see for people like us who are living outside [in the diaspora]? We are intellectuals, we work with ideas at universities. What role do you see for us in the revolution?" He remembers that Arafat looked at him quizzically and replied, "Doctor, when we began our revolution we didn't ask anyone. We were Palestinians sitting in Kuwait or Qatar thinking, what can we do for Palestine? We decided to make a revolution... It is for you to decide how to contribute to this revolution, which is yours."[6]

As the group got up to leave, Arafat hugged him and told him he should attend the special meeting of the Palestine National Council in Amman. My father had read about it in the newspapers but it never occurred to him that he could attend. At that meeting in Amman in the summer of 1970, however, the tension on the street was palpable as he walked with some old friends towards the meeting hall. The Jordanian army with its armored personnel carriers stood face to face with the Palestinian resistance fighters; it was unclear who was protecting whom from what. He was afraid that the Jordanians planned to surround and slaughter those gathered for the meeting, and his apprehensions at that time were well-founded—this was just before Black September when the armed Palestinian resistance was driven out. It was a decisive time for the

Palestinian armed struggle, betrayed and forced to move to Lebanon, only to be expelled again twelve years later by the Israeli invasion of 1982.

It was also a decisive moment for him personally. My father says he had a strong reaction to the meeting[7]:

> This was the very first time I had ever attended anything—official, unofficial, or popular—called Palestinian. Since 1948. Arab yes, with Palestinians, yes, but something Palestinian? I was so happy, so thrilled, even though this was the worst meeting, a terrible moment, and the tensions were unbelievable... But for the first time I truly saw my people. They talked just the way I did, we chattered and talked, and we kissed and hugged each other.

What was so incredible to him was that there was no other topic except Palestine. Everything was discussed in terms of its impact on Palestinians:

> And then in the evening, you'd sit and eat Palestinian foods... Foods I'd forgotten!

In a dramatic conclusion to the narrative he told his young admirer, he said:

> I had found my identity. I became part of the movement... My loyalty was now with the resistance. Nasser died and I shifted my affection to Arafat. I became a full-time functioning Palestinian.

To say that my father became fully Palestinian then is not to say that his cultural identity as a Palestinian had not always been central, or that he had not cared about the land of Palestine. My mother says that his deepest fear was that if they did not have their land, the Palestinians would end up like the Armenians or the Native Americans. He had long made analogies between Israel and other settler colonial states in North America, Africa and Australia and had even published a book on the comparison.[8]

My father explained to his interviewer, Hisham Ahmed-Fararjeh, that he didn't talk to his children about what had actually happened in 1948 as much as about Palestine, about his family: who he was and who his parents were. Indeed, he was glad that we lived in the Arab world in those early years. When we lived in Egypt in the late 1950s, we knew our Palestinian relatives there, his maternal aunt and a cousin's family with whom we were extremely close. Our grandmother often came to stay and, even after moving back to the US in 1960, we frequently went to Amman where at least I, the eldest, felt at home with the whole extended family. We always stayed with his mother, sister and his brother's large family who all lived together in a few rooms. We laid out mattresses on the floor at night, picked grapes off the arbor, and ate wonderful food. I sewed dolls' clothes in the old storeroom with my cousin, fell off a swing, went for Quran lessons, and had crushes on the boys next door (a family from Jaffa, of course).

I don't remember anything of what my father insists was his other important way of binding his children to Palestine. He tells his interviewers in Beirut that before 1967 we would go to Amman and then visit Jerusalem.

> What I was doing was, first I was tying my kids to our whole big tribe, uncles, aunts, cousins. They knew that I had relatives, that we were all Palestinians. But the second thing is that I was always determined to take them to Jerusalem. We'd rent the car and we'd go. This is our country. In Tulkarem we'd go to a high place and I'd say, "There, there's my home." You could see Jaffa, you could see the sea from there.

This was before the Israeli occupation of the West Bank.

As the daughter of a 1948 refugee who never herself experienced expulsion and grew up mostly in the US and with an American mother, my most intimate sense of belonging to Palestine consisted not in any connection to this territory that meant so much to him, but in the embodied closeness to relatives who shared my name and who gave me a childhood taste for special foods and an ear for a familiar dialect. The limits of my belonging came in moments like those, much later, when I learned that the language that filled my young life as my father talked affectionately to friends on the phone or argued political points was a dialect specific to Jaffa, the city of his birth and dreams of return. How would I know that?

But even if I had not had these childhood tastes and memories of family, there would still be no way not to be drafted into being Palestinian. You see the news of terrible events affecting other Palestinians and know that they are connected to you, somehow. You carry a name that raises eyebrows. When I was young, people often asked where my father was from. Before the hijackings of the 1960s that made Palestinians famous, people sometimes were puzzled by my answer. "Pakistan?" they would ask. Later, one would encounter strong views about Palestinians. Living elsewhere than among Palestinians both in the US and in Egypt, I would see myself through the eyes of others. Sometimes this meant bathing in support, sympathy and solidarity. This happened often in Egypt. In the US, it is different. The lies one reads lash the flesh and one is constantly stunned by what people say and believe. Blind to the everyday violence of checkpoints, imprisonment, racism and death; complicit in the rhetoric of retaliation and security; silent about the primal injustice of 1948 even when, in the best case, they are righteous about opposition to the Occupation or the settlements. To be a Palestinian in America is to learn to navigate this chasm in understandings of the world, to feel the hostility. For much of my life, being Palestinian could be put in the background. The luxury of the diaspora. The fruits of being second generation. The consequences of being mixed. But it was always there, to be managed.

For the generation that lost Palestine things are different. My father's younger brother, Said, now approaching eighty, confessed recently that he harbors a new hope that he'll be chosen among the 100,000 Palestinians that rumor has it the Palestinian Authority bargained could retain the right of return. He insists he'd move to Jaffa in a minute. He says simply, "I love it." My father's cousin, the relative we'd been so close to in Egypt and who then went to America, now lives in Amman. Widowed, she wanted to live near her brother and sister. She shares this longing for Palestine. She sang for us one day:

I'm a wounded bird
Living in the world, a stranger...
I search, for my country
But I have nothing but my laments...[9]

These are relatives we loved as children, who wanted us to know, to make us Palestinian. They were not, like my father, political. It was only after my father's death that I discovered that their attachments to Palestine and their sense of exile were as deep as his.

It was his mother again who my father would invoke in his stories of political commitment to suggest later his political independence from Arafat, despite the flattery and his own loyalty to the cause. My father liked to present his mother as radical. She read the newspaper, he said, as he did, though I remember her in her later years more often sitting on her bed cross-legged and reading the Quran. Her husband had taught her this habit when they married. My father got a kick out of telling people that she supported the more radical Popular Front for the Liberation of Palestine, though it was only because she liked George Habash, its leader, because she knew him personally and admired the fact that, as a physician, he had generously treated the refugees for free. But my grandmother was also more cautious than my father about politics. She talked politics in a whisper; she had seen her husband jailed by the British, one son shot dead in Tel Aviv, and her eldest son later jailed in Jordan, then exiled to Kuwait. My father insists, though, that she never stopped them from working for the liberation of Palestine.

"As a Palestinian," my father would explain, "you can't escape politics." He had thrown himself into it. What that meant had shifted over his lifetime. From the demonstrations against the British to the humiliations of finding himself a politicized refugee; from pouring himself into research and scholarly writing about the Arab world and the Palestine question to his passion for the visions of national liberation shared in the 1960s by anti-colonial and anti-imperialist groups across the Third World. From the brutality of the Israeli bombardment of the captive Palestinian population of Beirut during the Israeli invasion of Lebanon in 1982 (when he refused my mother's frantic offers to try to get him evacuated as an American) to the violence he witnessed in the Occupied Territories when he moved back—violence that made him (only partly tongue in cheek) urge disarmament of the whole Middle East as the only solution to the conflict.

When I met him at the airport in New York after he had survived the siege of Beirut in the summer of 1982, he was shaken. He had gone to set up an Open University for Palestinians and instead encountered a cluster bomb on his balcony. He seemed hollowed out. He had seen things that he didn't want to talk about with me. When he started lecturing and writing again, he said he had concluded that, "the question of Palestine cannot be answered through violence."[10] He was sobered by the damage that the Israelis caused to both the Palestinians and the Lebanese. "They had weapons of incredible power: bombs, cluster bombs and all sorts of weapons of destruction."

My father began to lecture in the 1980s about the impasse. His message: the Israeli military would never produce the surrender of the Palestinian people. He was right: the two Intifadas were still to come. But he also insisted that the opposite was equally true: no matter how much power the Palestinians might acquire, they would never produce the surrender of the Israelis. "They cannot impose their will and we cannot impose ours. Therefore, we have to figure out a way to reach a solution that both people can live with."[11]

Never one for introspection, my father had little patience for people who "looked at their bellybuttons," something he teased his

American children for doing. He always looked outward, whatever the personal cost to himself or to those close to him. He spoke, he wrote, he edited books, he started a publishing company in our house, he attended meetings and conferences. He traveled. If he told his friend, Edward Said, in his last days that, "In the end, there's only family," he had not lived his life as if this were so. He lived for Palestine, demanding that my mother live in its shadow. Then he left his marriage to return to Palestine. His children's visits with him became more difficult to manage, though he kept close to us and to the grandchildren he adored. He was driven by his conviction that people—as individuals and together—could shape the world, make things happen, change history. He created organizations from nothing. He was bent on realizing his dreams for Palestine, even if they kept being dashed.

Yet everyone who knew him intimately knew that my father was always haunted by another kind of dream. "The truth is," he told some liberal Zionist colleagues at Northwestern who always wanted to discuss "peace" and the situation "over there" with him, "I don't dream. All people dream, but not me. I have only one dream that recurs: a nightmare." Commenting to his interviewers in Beirut in 1982 that he had had this nightmare regularly since 1948, he continued the story of his conversation with his Northwestern colleagues:

> The dream never changes. And I have no other. Always, I am living by the sea—the house I grew up in was in Jaffa, right by the sea. A thief comes, a burglar. He starts pushing open the door and I try to shut it. A struggle that doesn't end. He pushes and I try to shut the door… And I scream but no one hears me. I'm shouting to the people in the house that someone's breaking in, but no one hears.

Even without understanding much about psychiatry (for which he had no patience), he said it isn't hard to interpret this dream. This is the Palestinian experience. "The struggle," he added, "is never resolved; the door always remains half-open."

He did what he could in his lifetime. After his death, I began to feel, hesitantly at first, that I had to take his place at the door. But how? Without his charisma and his passion for politics, I could not expect to inspire. Political argument makes me feel helpless. Defiant cultural expression—hip-hop groups from the ghettoes of Lyd who sing about who the real terrorists are; graffiti artists who paint on the Wall; eloquent poets whose language sears—thrills me. Yet I'm ambivalent about angry modes of political action, even though I sympathize with the sentiments.

In part this is because I live in the US and am forced to see Palestinians through the eyes of others. I take my children to demonstrations in New York and Washington when there is a crisis. I feel gratified when I find people walking side by side with Palestinians. I feel moments of discomfort when I'm overtaken by unshaven young men with green headbands waving Palestinian flags and shouting angry slogans about spirit and blood. I know they have relatives who have been killed or maimed. I know they may have grown up in refugee camps. I admire their passion but I know that I don't have to live, as they or my father did, as a "full time Palestinian," even if my attachments are real. (And my daughter's attachment strong enough to make her want to play for the Palestinian National Women's Soccer Team when she turned eighteen.) What I long for is a presentation of the truth of our story that can convince the kinds of people I know in the US who do not know what we know.

I was overcome by a calm determination when I finally found my voice. It came through a welcome invitation from someone I met at my father's funeral. We ended up working together with other scholars on a book, poignant and truthful, about the event that has defined Palestinians as a people who could not be at home. *Nakba: Palestine, 1948, and the Claims of Memory* was a work of mourning and a labor of love, rooted in the way I want to be Palestinian.[12] I was taking my father's place at the door, while he rests by the sea in Jaffa.

*Author's Note:* Portions of this essay have been published as "Forced Entry," a Birzeit University Working Paper 2011/27 (ENG) in the Conferences & Public Events Module and will be published in *Ibrahim Abu-Lughod and the Engaged Intellectual: Resurrecting a Model,* edited by Asem Khalil and Roger Heacock (Ibrahim Abu-Lughod Institute for International Studies, Birzeit University, 2012). This essay would have been impossible to write without the contributions of many. My greatest debt is to Hisham Ahmed-Fararjeh, who conducted an extraordinary series of interviews with my father in 1999 and 2000. He edited and published these in his book, *Ibrahim Abu-Lughod: Resistance, Exile and Return: Conversations with Hisham Ahmed-Fararjeh.* He also made available to the family the recordings of the original interviews and I have drawn heavily on them. Reja-e Busaileh generously shared with me the tapes of a long interview in Arabic with my father in Beirut in August 1982. Roger Nab'aa and Dominique Roch are listed as having translated and edited the interview, "Fragments d'une mémoire palestinienne," as it appeared in French in 1984. I have drawn on the original oral interviews to supplement the written texts, hoping to capture my father's zest for storytelling. I am grateful to my mother, sisters and brother for contributions, to Ahmad Harb and Roger Heacock for their insights into my father's role at Birzeit, and to Elaine Hagopian, who recorded her own astute and affectionate memories in two articles that appeared in the *Arab Studies Quarterly,* the journal my father helped found. Finally, Mark Levine gave me good comments on a much earlier version that he inspired me to write. I am grateful to him for his respect for my father, with whom he shared a passion for Jaffa, and for his understanding of my own political sensitivities.

### Notes

[1] Hisham Ahmed-Fararjeh, *Ibrahim Abu-Lughod: Resistance, Exile and Return: Conversations with Hisham Ahmed-Farajeh* (Ibrahim Abu-Lughod Institute for International Studies, Birzeit University, 2003).

[2] Mahmoud Darwish, "Ibrahim Abu-Lughod: The Path of Return is the Path of Knowledge," Eulogy, Qasaba Theatre, Ramallah, May 26, 2001. Translated for the family by Tania Tamari Nasir.

[3] Ibrahim Abu-Lughod, "Fragments d'une mémoire palestinienne," *Revue d'études palestiniennes,* 10 (1984).

[4] Hisham Ahmed-Fararjeh, op.cit.

[5] Ibid.

[6] Ibid.

[7] Ibid.

[8] Ibrahim Abu-Lughod and Baha Abu-Laban (eds.), *Settler Regimes in Africa and the Arab World: The Illusion of Endurance* (Wilmette, IL: Medina University Press International, 1974).

[9] Shahla Abu-Lughod Nakib composed this song.

[10] Ibrahim Abu-Lughod, "The Meaning of Beirut," *Race & Class*, 24/4 (1982).

[11] Hisham Ahmad Fararjeh, op.cit.

[12] Ahmad H. Sa'di and Lila Abu-Lughod (eds.), *Nakba: Palestine, 1948, and the Claims of Memory* (New York: Columbia University Press, 2007). My own essay, "Return to Half-Ruins: Memory, Postmemory, and Living History in Palestine," was a kind of mourning.

# ADANIA SHIBLI

## Of Place, Time and Language

### Little Girls of Jenin

I feel happiness, like a light, gentle pressure on the bones of my chest, while the rest of my body has vanished into languor. I don't find it foolish, as happiness usually is, but, rather, strong and persistent; a happiness that doesn't doubt itself, not even for a second.

And the reason for this happiness is that I'm going to give a reading at the Jenin refugee camp. My happiness is certain that, and because, its source is the desire to put an end to pain; to prevent pain from continuing to monopolize my soul, as it has for some years now, after my first and last visit to the camp in the spring of 2002, even though Jenin itself is the city of my childhood.

As a little girl, I used to accompany my father during his visits there every Friday. I would observe the shops and the colorful items dangling from their ceilings. The scene dearest to my heart was that of watching a shop owner bring down one of those items. With the light-handedness of a magician, while still engaged in conversation with a client, he'd lower the ball or the money box from above with the help of a rod that had a hook at one end. And I, the little person down at the other end, would think until that moment that only birds could touch those items dangling from Jenin's sky.

As I grew up, my cities grew with me, while Jenin remained little. I didn't visit it except in transit, on my route from Jerusalem or Ramallah to my village near Jenin, traveling to visit my family. However, since the closing and blocking of roads and the spread of checkpoints in 2000, it had become impossible for Palestinian cars to use that route, and I could no longer travel on it. But now, in this spring, seven years later, I will do so as a passenger in a German diplomatic car.

I try to recall the sections of that road that are dearest to my eyes but the choice is difficult. As a final compromise I select a section between Nablus and Jenin, where the road bends to the right and then slopes down. There, in that curve, some almond trees are hiding, overlooking vast fields of wheat. Suddenly, I'm struck by a filthy fear and I don't know how it has found its way to me: what if those trees are no longer there? Seven years are a long time, during which thousands of lives were terminated, thousands of homes destroyed, and thousands of acres confiscated. And thousands of trees were uprooted. A slight pain is back, dismantling the pleasant pressure in my chest, denying me a measure of happiness. So I summon up a feeling of indifference, brushing aside both feelings of pain and happiness. And, holding on to my indifference, I tell myself that maybe those three or four almond trees are still there or maybe they're not.

I then start thinking about what I should wear. A black shirt that I love a lot, given to me as a gift by my brother, and new light-brown pants I bought recently. Now the shoes. I try to imagine the ground I'll be walking on. The only time I was in the camp the ground consisted of rubble. I remember the shoes I wore during that visit in the spring of 2002. I hate those shoes immensely. After that visit I threw them away, together with all the destruction they stepped on. I never talk about that visit. I can't and I won't and I don't care to or maybe it tires me or ruins me to talk about it or even to write about how I can't talk about it. Briefly put, it is a visit not to be repeated, not even in words. But I remind myself again that this time I'm going to the camp as a guest writer, and not in the company of blood-sucking journalists. I choose a pair of elegant black shoes. But in no time I become the prey of a new fear. What if the road to Jenin is still paved with destruction? I imagine being forced to climb mountains in order to avoid the checkpoints or roadblocks that will stand in my way. I even imagine the bullet that will pierce my body. I assign its place. It will either be in my leg or in my chest. And though I prefer it to be in my leg, I say that if it hits my chest and I die, there's nothing to it. There's nothing to lose in this ghastly world, except for entering Jenin camp today. Then, in anticipation of all the perils and hardships I imagine standing in my way, I put a shoe brush and black shoe polish in my bag. I want to stand in front of the audience of Jenin camp wearing a clean, shining pair of shoes even if it is over my dead body.

We arrive at the camp. I don't recognize anything in it or in its alleys. The death that hung over it five years ago, to the day, has been lifted by an ordinary, everyday, languid afternoon. Two men sit outside a poultry shop, while a little kid pushes a pink pram onto the street. Suddenly, I scream loudly as I imagine the wheels of the car we are in running him over. The smell of death hits my nose—it's nested forever in this square.

The reading will start shortly in the Freedom Theater that has recently been opened in the camp. Young people fill the yard outside it. At the entrance, I run into a group of little girls, their arms crossed, fury in their eyes. I ask, "What's wrong, pretty ones?" And they reply that the man at the door will not let them in. In their furious eyes I spot a glimpse of my childhood in Jenin. They want to go in, and I'm the little girl with them, to where the adults, including me, will be. I talk to the theater director, begging him to allow the girls in, but he insists, "No." He says the event isn't meant for their age group and they would only cause a commotion inside. The girls and I assure him that we will be orderly and will sit quietly at the back, but he still refuses.

I go back to the little girls and promise them, from the bottom of my heart, that I will come back to Jenin just for them and that we won't admit any adults into the theater. But they look at me with eyes that have neither patience nor trust, for how many promises have been showered on them and on their parents and grandparents before! Before I enter the theater, I hear them screaming at the door-keeper from a distance, "We will enter, we will!"

They do not know that they have, instead, entered my weary soul and breathed new life into it, true life.

*Spring 2007*

## Out of Time

My little watch is the first to sense the change, going into and out of Palestine. On the way there, I notice it on my wrist, counting the time down to the second, waiting for the moment when the wheels of the plane touch the runway and I set it to local time, which it counts with an infinite familiarity. Then, as soon as I leave Palestine, my watch advances listlessly, taking its time parting with the local time there, which only vanishes when the plane touches down in a foreign land.

It may seem to some that I'm slightly exaggerating what I'm saying about my watch, especially as it is very tiny. People are often amazed that it can tell me the time at all, being so tiny. I myself would have shared their doubts had I not found out about watches and their secret powers, as I did.

It goes back to primary school, during one of the Arabic literature classes. The curriculum back then was, and still is, subject to the approval of the Israeli Censorship Bureau, which allowed teaching texts from various Arab countries, bar Palestine, fearing that they would contain references or even suggestions that could raise the pupils' awareness of the Palestine Question. Hence, Palestinian literature was considered unlawful, if not taboo, similar to pornography. Except for one text, *The Time and Man*, a short story by Samira Azzam, which the Censorship Bureau had found "harmless."

The story, published in 1963, is about a young man getting ready to turn in the night before his very first day at work. He sets his alarm for four o'clock in the morning so as to catch the train in time to get to work. No sooner did the alarm go off the next morning, than there was a knocking at his front door. When he opened it, he found an old man in front of him. He had no clue who this man was and he did not get a chance to ask him, because the man turned and walked away, disappearing into the darkness. This was repeated day after day, so that the young man no longer set the alarm. It was only several months later that he discovered who the old man was, after a colleague told him this man went knocking on the doors of all the employees of the company. He would wake them up in order for them not to be late for their trains and meet the same fate as his own son. His son had arrived late at the station one morning, just as the train was leaving. He held onto its door, but his hand betrayed him and he slipped, falling under the wheels of the train.

At first glance, this story might seem simple and safe, especially to the censor's eyes. But it contributed to shaping my consciousness regarding Palestine as no other text I have ever read has done. Were there once Palestinian employees who commuted to work by train? Was there a train station? Was there once a train whistling in Palestine? Was there ever once a normal life in Palestine? So where is it now and why has it vanished?

The text engraved in my soul a deep yearning for all that had been, including the normal, the banal and the tragic, to such an extent that I could no longer accept the marginalized, minor life to which we've been exiled since 1948, when our existence turned into a "problem."

Against this story and the multiple modes of existence it revealed to me, stands my little watch. And my watch is more like that old man in Azzam's story than a Swiss watch whose primary concern is to count time with precision. Rather, just as the old man turned from a human being into a watch in order for life to become bearable, so did my watch decide to turn from a watch into a human being.

In Palestine, my watch often stops moving. It suddenly goes into a coma, unable to count time. On my last visit there, I set it, as usual, to local time the minute the plane touched down at Lyd Airport. It was ten-to-two in the afternoon. I headed towards passport control. There weren't many travelers and the line I stood in was proceeding quickly. I handed my passport over to the police officer and she took her time looking at it. Then more time. Suddenly, two men and a woman appeared, a mix of police, security and secret services. They took me out of the line and began a long process of questioning and searches. Everything proceeded as usual in such situations: an exhaustive interrogation into the smallest details of my life and a thorough search of my belongings. Afterwards, I was led into a room for a body search and, while one woman walked away with my shoes and belt to x-ray them, another stayed behind with my watch, which she held in her palm, contemplating it with great intent and devotion. After a few minutes, she looked at her watch, then back at mine. And again at her watch, then at mine. When the first woman came back with the rest of my belongings, she hurried over to tell her that there was something very strange about my watch. It was not moving. Five minutes had passed according to her watch, whereas according to mine, none had. They called the security chief and my heart started to bang violently in my chest.

I don't know how much time passed before my watch, and then I, were cleared of all suspicions and allowed to leave. But I discovered when I reached home that it was nine o'clock in the evening, while my watch was still pointing to ten-to-two in the afternoon. Perhaps my watch was trying to comfort me by making me believe that all that searching and delay had lasted zero minutes. That nothing had happened. Or maybe it simply refuses to count the time that is seized from my life, time whose only purpose is to humiliate me and drive me to despair; a suspension of time that is intended for the obstruction of pain.

Contrary to this malfunctioning in Palestine, my watch has not once stopped outside it. It is never late when counting every second of this other time. In fact, it often moves faster than it should, to a point where it seems to lose track of time altogether. It moves fast, as if wanting to shake off this other time from the dial, one second after the other, in order to catch up with the time in Palestine.

Thus, whether seven hours or zero away from Palestine, my little watch comforts me, by leading me out of time, no matter where I am.

*Autumn 2006*

## The Load of Language

I look at a picture of a hillside marked by those low stone walls that divide it into evenly spaced terraces, so as to allow the olive trees to grow with the least possible effort. This picture depicts one of the most familiar scenes in Palestine, so familiar that there was no reason to look at it with such attention as I did that night. This may not have been the case had I not just returned to my house from a dinner party at a restaurant in an old neighborhood in Seoul. Vast tin pots stuffed with pepper and sesame plants stood next to huge jars, huge enough to allow Aladdin to hide in them, but for now they were filled with sauces and fermented food. Such tin pots and jars were neatly arranged all over the place: down alleys, in doorways, on balconies, and over the low rooftops.

On leaving the neighborhood to sink silently into the darkness, I decided to take the bus instead of the subway home. The bus arrived even before I had finished bowing to my friends. I climbed on quickly and sat on a seat by the window at the back, where I let my eyes be dragged into the night of Seoul. Streets scribbled with headlights, young men and women coming and going on the pavements, the brash colors of neon signs flickering nonstop, making the city look like a jukebox in the corner of a pub.

So when I arrived home and saw that picture, I, suddenly terrified, realized how far away I was. Over the past five years, after leaving Palestine, hillsides like these have disappeared from my sight. I realized this only tonight, here. Such scenery, of which my existence was an indivisible part for so many years, is now out of reach. I am outside it.

From such a distance, I hasten to look for what may have remained with me, despite my leaving. Even the ground cardamom, which I had insisted on keeping with me, as it somehow kept me attached to people and places there, I have recently stopped carrying—its small particles seemed to grow too heavy for me. Finally, all I find is words.

For a wanderer like myself, whose primary concern is to possess as little as possible so as to carry as little as possible, only words are left. Words that have no weight, no size, no smell; quiet, invisible, intangible, they are all that I can carry in my ceaseless wandering from one city to another. Words, though, are able to do what stones do in the walls in that picture of a hillside. In all sizes and all shapes, small and large, heavy and light, they come together to turn a strange land into a land I can inhabit, with the least possible effort.

*Autumn 2008*

"Little Girls of Jenin" *was translated from Arabic by the author;* "Out of Time" *by Suneela Mobayi;* and "The Load of Language" *by* Babelmed *magazine.*

# HOME/EXILE

My Country:
Close to Me as My Prison

Go to Haifa and play soccer with the
first Palestinian boy you see on the
street.

I have never been there, unfortunately, but
you bet it will be the first place I go to, if and
when, I get my American passport. If I go to
Israel, and my passport shows that I have
been there, it would limit my ability to visit
my family in Lebanon which is a must at the
moment.

- Hana
Born in Beirut, living in Houston, TX
Lebanese Passport
Father and Mother from Haifa
(both exiled in 1948)

Notes: I played soccer with a boy named Kamel in the Halisa
neighborhood of Haifa.

إذهبي إلى حيفا و العبي كرة القدم مع أول
ولد فلسطيني تربنه في الطريق.

للأسف لم أذهب إلى هناك أبدا، و لكن بالتأكيد،
ستكون فلسطين أول مكان أذهب إليه إذا ما
حصلت على جواز سفر أمريكي. إذا ذهبت إلى
إسرائيل وظهر هذا في جواز سفري، فإن هذا
سيحد من إمكانية زيارة عائلتي في لبنان،
و هذا أمر ضروري جدا في الوقت الحاضر.

- هناء
من مواليد بيروت، و تعيش في هيوستن، تكساس
مواطنة لبنانية
الأب والأم من حيفا
(نفيا عام ١٩٤٨)

ملاحظات: لعبت كرة القدم مع ولد إسمه كامل في منطقة الطليصة
في حيفا.

# SUAD AMIRY

## An Obsession

### I. Would You Ever Let Go of Me?

*My country: close to me as my prison*—Mahmoud Darwish

Would you *ever* let go of me
For a lifetime
For a year
A month
An hour
A minute
Even a second?

No

If *ever*
If ever we get an apology
If ever we get compensation for our losses
It would not be about a lost country
It would not be about a lost field
Or an orange grove
Or a lost home

## An Obsession

No

It would not be about the hundreds of bulldozed villages
Or the shattering of a whole society
It would not be about losing a livelihood
A stolen piano, a Persian carpet or a first baby photo album
And it would not be about someone's personal library
A left-behind Arab horse or a Cypriot donkey
Nor a Persian cat nor even Shasa, the monkey that my mother gave
  me a few days before the war

No

And it would not be about the blooming almond trees and the red
  flowering pomegranates that were *not* tenderly picked in the
  spring of 1948 nor in the summer after
And it would not be about firing on the farmers who returned to
  harvest the fields they left behind
Nor would it be about the many deserted budding roses
Or a bride's wardrobe and her many cherished presents
Or a child or an old woman who was forgotten, left behind in the
  midst of havoc

No

It would not be about concealing a crime or falsifying history
It would not be about blaming the victim
It would not be about dehumanizing and stereotyping
It would not be about making new "wandering Jews" out of us
It would not be about reversing roles and images

No

If at all
It will *only* be about an *obsession*

### Yes, an Obsession

My dreams are all about you
And my nightmares are all because of you
My happiness is related to you
And my sadness comes from you
My expectations are all concerning you
And my disappointments pile up beside you

Yes

And if I run away, I run away from you
And if I come back, I come back to you
If I love someone, it is because of what they think of you
And if I hate someone, it is because of what they say about you

Yes

And it is because of you:
Nothing in my life is normal
Nothing in my life is neutral
Nothing is mundane
Or even insignificant

### And how very *exhausting* it is

O how I desire one ordinary day when you do not haunt me
How I long for a pleasant evening where you are not invited
Yearn for amnesia from you
How I wish for a stroke that
will neatly delete everything related to you:
Thoughts, memories, emotions
Gone forever

I heard them moan for you before I was born
And I heard them moan for you after I was born and ever since I
    was born

An Obsession

Their bedtime stories are about you
And their daydreaming is also about you
I've seen them cry, laugh, praise and curse

You, You, and only YOU
I had to learn everything about you
I had to imagine you from across a border
Miss you
Love you
Defend you
Cry for you
Write about you
Talk about you
And, in command form, love you

And how very *exhausting* it is

Above all I have to keep my sanity with all the brutality around you
Every hour, every minute and every second
If ever I do come to terms with what has happened to you
I must banish that part of my brain
That cherishes reason, logic, justice

Palestine

Will you ever set me free?


## II. Where Do You Come From? Multiple Choice Answers to Questions about My Life

I can hardly think of a day or a week that passes without someone, somewhere, enquiring: are you married? Do you have children? Where do you come from?

This happens much more frequently when one is on the road

and, since I have been traveling for most of my life, I have become quite skilful in my responses. I use various ones depending on the occasion, my mood, and how long I want the conversation to last.

*Are you married?*

If I am lucky and happen to encounter a *handsome* man (at my age I am embarrassed to say a *young* and handsome man), just to keep my options open my response(s) include:

"Yes, sort of," with a soft *yes* and an accentuated *sort of.*

"Yes, but," with an ambiguous *yes* and a clear *but.*

"I have a part-time husband," with an English mumble, eating the *husband* (I mean the word, not my husband), but with full enunciation of *part-time.*

In all three responses, the story, for good or bad, starts or finishes right there.

*Do you have children?*

This wins as the most frequently asked question and it takes a more exact formulation in the Arab world: "How *many* children do you have?"

Unlike the marriage question, the children question is rather innocent and is often asked simply to start a friendly but rather mundane conversation. I have often thought how much more exciting the conversation would be if it were slightly altered:

"Are you married?"
"No."
"Do you have children?"

But unfortunately this rarely happens. The most you can wish for nowadays is for people to be politically correct (sexually correct) and ask if you have a partner, which leaves a margin for speculation and a bit of imagination.

Back to children. If I am not exactly in the mood for, "What a pity" (*haram*) or "Poor thing" (*miskeeneh*) or "Really! Why? Is it you or your husband?" with an emphasis on the husband, I simply lie:

Lie Number 1: "Yes, I have one daughter."

If in Italy, this is enough to end the conversation by saying in my bad Italian: "*Si, ho una figlia.*" However, rest assured that the response in the Arab world would be: "Only one girl? May God give you a taste of boys" (*Allah yet'amek awlad*), with an emphasis on the wrong sex (girl) and the wrong number (one).

It will also entail a long conversation, full of sympathy, but most importantly, with a long list of fail-safe fertility doctors and hospitals. And, if the conversation takes place with a taxi driver in Amman or Cairo, the probability of being driven to the fertility doctor or infertility clinic right away is extremely high. If I had listened to taxi drivers' advice, I would probably have had four or five kids by now.

Lie Number 2: "*Alhamdulellah*, thank God, I have two boys," I lie with a straight face. But this time, since the sex is right, the emphasis will be on the number: "Only two?"

Lie Number 3: If I strike the right balance of sex and number by answering, "I have a boy and a girl," then the response is bound to be: "Don't you want a brother for your only son?" Never mind a sister for my daughter.

Indeed, going full tilt and claiming two daughters and four sons may be the very best response for ending a conversation in the Arab world: "May God keep them for you, marry them well, and give you the taste of grandchildren." End of story. Although, such a large number of children would probably extend, rather than end, the conversation in China (population anxiety) or Europe (immigration anxiety).

I was around thirty-eight, with a ticking biological clock, when I went to visit Abu Ahmad, the owner of a stone factory in the industrial zone of Al-Bireh, Ramallah's twin city. I wanted to conclude an agreement with him about the type, quality and quantity of stone I needed for a housing project I was building.

My visit to his factory started with Arabic coffee with lots of cardamom and hardly any coffee, and a glass of cold water that quenched my August thirst. Abu Ahmad always had many medium-sized jars of honey in his office. Like his stones, the different types and colors of his honey were of superb quality. Somehow, Abu Ahmad seemed more keen on selling his honey than the huge stone blocks. Certainly, he spent far more time explaining the great benefits of honey to me and others. I don't really understand the connection between honey and Islam, but I have noticed that many pious Muslims or "preachers" sell honey.

Shortly after his detailed lecture on honey, Abu Ahmad and I ventured out to his vast stone-yard to discuss my substantial order. I was in the midst of four or five stonemasons, totally absorbed in explaining the desired texture of stone to each of them—I wanted the half-dressed stone called *mfagiar* (literally meaning "the exploded"), not the roughly-dressed stones called *tubzeh* ("rough"), nor the too finely-dressed ones called *misamsam* ("from sesame")— when I heard Abu Ahmad's enquiry: "Doctora Suad, why didn't you bear children?" I couldn't believe my ears. Was I dreaming? Who was hallucinating, Abu Ahmad or I?

My face froze but my eyes moved nervously left, right and center among the five stonecutters and dressers. They had, meanwhile, also ceased their tick-tack-tick-tack stone, hammer and chisel symphony. I could see that it was not *only* Abu Ahmad who was interested in the reason why I had not borne any children so far. The key question—was it my fault or my husband's—seemed to be answered in the eyes around me: I definitely needed a "strong" husband (*fahel*). To get myself off the hook I had to quickly come up with a convincing reply to end the conversation and get back to stones: "Ya Haj Abu Ahmad, it is God's will!" (*Allah ma a'tana*, God did not give us.) As Abu Ahmad was a religious pilgrim, a Haj, I opted to put it down to my God-given destiny.

"Come on, Doctora Suad, I did not expect such an answer from an educated person like yourself—neither medicine nor science has left any room for God now," Abu Ahmad countered briskly. Wanting badly to end my embarrassment I said, "Okay, Abu Ahmad, I promise you I'll give both science and medicine a chance."

Leaving his stone factory, I thought, damn it, Abu Ahmad, you got me! But can you imagine my telling him the truth: that neither I nor my husband ever wanted children? They would all think we are crazy—and perhaps they are right.

And finally:

*Where do you come from?*

"Palestine." Period. Or is it?

Hmm... believe me, there is nothing normal about that simple response. This question is definitely time-consuming, politically stimulating, emotionally engaging and, more often than not, t-r-o-u-b-l-e...

You cannot simply admit that you are from "Palestine" or "Palestinian"—like saying I am American or I am French or Indian—and expect to be left alone or to receive a standard reply: "Oh, really, India—that's nice, I would love to go there one day." Or, "Ah, India! Bollywood, ha ha ha."

No, you cannot expect to utter the word Palestine and simply walk away. You are either drowned in a flood of sympathy or, even worse, find yourself in a seminar on *the conflict*.

Where do you come from when you are the daughter of a Palestinian father who, like the rest of the 850,000 Palestinians, was forced out of his homeland in 1948? The whole CV: born in Damascus of a Syrian mother, raised in Amman until I was seventeen, spent a total of another eleven years between Cairo, Beirut, Ann Arbor and Edinburgh. Until 1981, when I came to Palestine for a six-month visit that has lasted thirty years.

So—am I from Jaffa? From Amman? From Damascus or from Ramallah?

And am I from Palestine? A "stateless" place declared a "state" in 1947, 1988, 1993 and, once again, in September 2011—a stateless place lost on its own ground, that has been seeking "recognition" for the last sixty-some years.

And in our last attempt in September 2011, our "President" was reprimanded by Barack Obama, as well as by many European countries for seeking a UN resolution—exactly the same way Israel was created in 1947. Our stateless state is now under tremendous pressure (along with poor Bosnia) to face-save the powerful United States so that it is not "forced" to use its veto power in the Security Council. I can't help but recall Golda Meir's famous statement: "I resent the Palestinians for forcing us to kill them."

To top it all, President Obama accused our "President," Abu Mazen, of trying to take a "short cut." If negotiating with the Israelis for the last twenty years (1991-2011), while enduring the building of Jewish settlements on 60 per cent of West Bank land, is called a "short cut," I would hate to see what a long cut will look like. So much for the "Audacity of Hope."

*So: where do you come from?*

Not wanting to be guilty-until-proven-innocent in the unwelcome company of airport security officials, I have developed several half-lies to get around the question in ordinary conversation.

Half-lie Number 1: If absolutely not in the mood to talk, I normally opt for the city or country in which I grew up: "I am from Amman." If the person seems to be at a total loss, I add: "Jordan!"

In most cases the conversation ends instantly. Then we move on to more exciting subjects. (Sorry, Jordan, much as I am indebted to you and love you, somehow you do not inspire interesting conversations.)

Half-lie Number 2: If in the mood for a historical discourse on the past (but certainly not today when President Bashar el Assad is massacring his people), I say: "I am from Damascus." This often gets you two responses:

"Ah! From Damascus, that must be a beautiful city."
"Yes, absolutely lovely," is my concise response to close the subject.

The other response is more difficult to finesse:

"Wow, really! What an absolutely splendid city... it's so authentic... also Aleppo and Palmyra. Wow! Syria is really beautiful."

Once I realize that the person happens to know much more about Damascus and Syria than I do, I try to change the subject. And if you are really curious about the reasons why, I will take the time to bore you and explain:

Like most Arab countries, Syria loves Palestine but hates the Palestinians, especially those who have been contaminated by the Occupation, once or twice. "Once" refers to Palestinians residing in the West Bank or the Gaza Strip who hold a pseudo-Palestinian passport; "twice" to the 1948 Palestinians who hold a real, but non-kosher Israeli passport. If a Palestinian passport holder (my category) stands a next-to-zero chance of getting to my beloved Syria, the other category is at nil. (But I must add that this is true of most Arab countries with the exception of Jordan.)

And then, try using your Palestinian "passport" at the world's gatekeeper, an international airline terminal.

*Departures*

"What prefix is Palestine?" asks the innocent airline company officer as he or she tries to puzzle out my passport.

"Try PNA, which stands for Palestinian National Authority," I say calmly as he jiggles his keyboard. "No," he shakes his head.

"Hmm, then try PA—Palestinian Authority—drop the National."
He punches his keyboard again. "Nothing."

"Try POT (Palestinian Occupied Territories)." "No."

"Get rid of the Occupation, try PT (Palestinian Territories)," I
laugh, a bit desperately. He keeps at it.

"Try DPT (Disputed Palestinian Territories)... Okay, perhaps not
Disputed, what about WBGS (West Bank and Gaza Strip)?" "No."

"WBGSJ (West Bank, Gaza Strip and Jerusalem)?" "No."

"Take out the J, the Eternal Capital for the Jewish People."
"Mmm."

He is silent; I am still at it.

"Try PS (Palestinian Stupidity)."

He coaxes his computer. "No." He tries for a long time and then
says, "Ah, okay, I found it, it's PSE."

"Great, PSE," I say with a big sigh, trying to figure out what is
Eternal in Palestinian Stupidity.

As the airline officer smiles at his successful decoding of this
weird document and hands me my boarding pass, I'm off like a
bullet to catch my flight.

While I am painfully aware that we, as a nation, have been
missing the train for the last sixty-three years, ever since they found
a land with no people for a people with no land, now, as holders
of this weird document, I feel we also run the risk of missing so
many planes.

*Arrivals*

In anticipation, I often feel the vibrations of the airport "security alert" as soon as I hand in my Arabic right-to-left passport (or,
as often described, writing in reverse). The minute the passport
control official flips the passport left to right I know it's trouble. And,
to add insult to injury, I hand him a passport that has no country,
but on which is written, first in Arabic, then in English:

## THE PALESTINIAN AUTHORITY
### Passport
*Travel Document*

It must have taken *the* Palestinians (I should say "Palestinians," because for years both the Israelis and the Americans have deprived us of the article *the*) and the Israelis days on end to agree on the size of the three fonts. If only Arafat had spent as much time on the Oslo Accords negotiating a settlements freeze, we would have had a real state and a real passport by now. But unfortunately he did not.

Once the passport control official gets over the initial alarm caused by this peculiar document, the rest is usually sorted out in a small, depressing interrogation room.

So much for my many answers to being a married Palestinian woman with no children.

# RAJA SHEHADEH

# Diary of an Internal Exile: Three Entries

## I. March 31, 2003

A misty day of slow-moving low fog. At noon, as the sun attempted to penetrate this gossamer veil that had fallen over Ramallah, I circled around the building that had once housed the Israeli military court and prison to see what remained. Perched on one of the highest hills of Ramallah, this rectangular British Mandate-built police fortress of reinforced concrete was constructed around an open inner courtyard. Commencing in 1938, the British built some fifty such structures in various parts of Palestine. They were initiated by Sir Charles Tegart, a former commissioner of police in Calcutta, who was sent to Palestine as a counterterrorism expert in the midst of the 1936 Palestinian popular revolt against Mandate rule.

His other inspirational ideas adopted by British Mandate officials were to build a security wall along the northern border of Palestine to prevent infiltration, to import Dobermann Pinschers from South Africa, and to establish a special center in Jerusalem to train interrogators in torture. Their heritage must have informed the guards and interrogators of this Israeli prison who used some of the same techniques: humiliation, beatings and severe physical maltreatment, including the Turkish practice of hitting prisoners on the soles of their feet and genitals. In appreciation of Sir Charles, these fortresses have since been known as Tegart Buildings.

Last spring, Israeli tanks and soldiers invaded Ramallah and other West Bank cities. Since then Israeli tanks and planes have been sporadically bombarding this fortress in which the President of the Palestinian Authority, Yasser Arafat, stubbornly held fast. There was some danger in getting close to the building, but this was not why I hesitated. I braced myself for the extent of destruction in a site that carries so much meaning for me. I stood peering through the fog, trying to make out what was left of it after the latest Israeli attack. An eerie silence prevailed and droplets of water saturated the heavy air.

There were piles of rubble from which twisted metal rods protruded. Slabs of thick cement sloped at a dangerous angle. The rear portion of the building still managed to stand, though sections of the wall had been shattered and columns severed from their base drooped like giant icicles. Some balconies of the once formidable bastion were still visible. Israeli soldiers would look down from these to the courtyard where other soldiers roamed and peeled their oranges as they sunned themselves after lunch. A nearby extension built by the Palestinian Authority and connected to the teetering structure in the back by a bridge was still intact. The southern wall of the toilet along the street where I was standing, used by Palestinians who had to wait for hours before being allowed to visit prisoners, was shattered, exposing the porcelain tiles which now formed a white seam bordering this section of the ruined building. A few Palestinian flags fluttered forlornly here and there. All that remained of this collapsing structure was veiled by the shroud of fog that seemed to wrap the hill on which the Tegart Building once stood.

Thirty-five years ago, the victorious Israeli army entered this British garrison, took it over from the Jordanian army and stationed itself here. Seven years ago, the army left the building, handing it over to the Palestinian leadership. Not long after this, Israeli tanks and planes returned to topple it over the heads of Arafat and his retinue. Still, the resilient Palestinians refuse to go. They continue, despite all the odds, to operate a shabby administration in the shambles of a destroyed tower.

Over the years, this Muqataa or compound, as we now called it, has acquired layers of meaning. It was where the hated Israeli military governor of Ramallah established his headquarters shortly after the June war in 1967. It was also the site of my legal battles, and those of many others, both in defense of political prisoners at the military court and in land cases where we attempted to but rarely succeeded in defeating the Israeli claim that Palestinian land fell into the category of public land and, consequently, belonged to the Jewish people. It was here that I first learned about torture from one of my clients, Khalid Ameerah, a young schoolboy, barely sixteen, and formulated my commitment to human rights; where I met those fighters for freedom, some mere children, some female university students, others seasoned militants, whose resilience and courage I came to admire and whom I was proud to defend. It was the place where many of my most formative experiences took place. The Tegart Building thus honed my character and made me the person I've become.

The Israeli war planes had bombarded the offices of the military prosecutor where I used to come to learn about new military orders that I then interpreted in my persistent attempt to fathom the nature of this Israeli Occupation and its particular brand of colonization. Also hit was the adjoining military court where I so often stood before a military judge and contested orders for the expropriation of land for the benefit of Jewish settlers, struggling to suppress my anxiety, wondering what the judge was feeling and thinking about what he was seeing around him. It was where I encountered hateful human beings as well as others who tried to respond humanely and offered help in ways that sometimes succeeded in easing the suffering. This court to which I came in the cold and the heat, in winter and summer, had never been just another building. Every corner was imbued with meaning and memories for me, as for many others, and now it was being shelled by those who had once used it to administer their warped sense of legal order. Not unlike what was being done to Palestine itself, those Israeli tanks and war planes were attempting to turn this bastion of meaning into a ruin, hidden behind a film of haze and milky-white fog.

How often during those years of struggle, as I waited in the corridors of power, had I dreamed of the day when I would see this symbol of injustice demolished, obliterated out of existence, blown to smithereens after those operating it had been sent home. And yet, in my apocalyptic fantasy, it was we, the aggrieved party, who would carry out this terminal action, not our oppressors with their planes and tanks. It was we who would be the perpetrators of this ritual of purification marking our victory over our oppressors. That vision meant a lot to me and sustained me during the darker stages of the struggle. But now, the partially destroyed structures shimmering behind a veil of fog attested to the power of the usurpers of our freedom to destroy not only our physical surroundings, but also the depositories of our dreams.

It was only in January 1996, when the Palestinian Authority was established, that this compound was opened to the general public for a very brief period of time. How different was that first viewing from this one. Then there were many people, some solemn, some celebratory, walking respectfully into the interrogation rooms, into the prison and into the courtrooms, accompanied by former prisoners who pointed out significant markers, places, objects and writings scrawled on the wall. There was such euphoria then, a sense of pride that the prison and torture chambers where so many suffered had been liberated. In reverent silence we followed the former prisoners who proudly guided us through the alleys of this labyrinthine structure, describing the suffering they had endured. Sometimes the memory of one of those who died under torture or in prison would surface and our guide would choke. We would stand in respectful silence, trying our best to imagine what none of us had had to endure. That stroll through the site of memories of those most aggrieved convinced me that I should abandon my apocalyptic fantasy. This place, I now thought, should be turned into a museum commemorating an important stage in the struggle waged from the Occupied Territories to resist the Israeli Occupation, just as the prisons of Khyyam in South Lebanon and Robben Island in South Africa had been after liberation.

I remember looking forward to the day when former detainees would accompany young Palestinians and recount the bitter but proud history of our embattled nation. But it was not to be. Events took a different turn. And now I peered through the fog at the ruins beyond, trying to determine which of them could still be salvaged and perhaps recreated.

Beyond the confines of the ruins of the Tegart, I looked at the fog-enveloped Ramallah hills. It was once possible to roam these hills and enjoy their pristine beauty. They served as my refuge when I was active as a litigation lawyer — I would go to them and shed the dreaded military Occupation. It always worked. Once in the hills, I would experience a sense of freedom that I didn't feel anywhere else in Ramallah. All that was over. Now many of the hills were out of reach, used by settlers, closed off by checkpoints, criss-crossed by roads, and made dangerous by gunfire. Just like this Tegart, the land of Palestine was undergoing a process of transformation that might one day render it unrecognizable to the very people who had lived in it their entire lives.

## II. November 16, 2004

Today I entered the Compound through the eastern gate on my way to give my condolences for the death of Yasser Arafat. His funeral had taken place three days earlier, after his body was brought back from a hospital in Paris. I came upon a wide open space which has been cleared by Palestinians of the large piles of rubble left after the Israeli army began demolishing the Muqataa. Of the four-sided structure built around an inner courtyard, only the northeastern segment, where Arafat had established his last office, was left standing. I stood before the building with metal beams protruding from its side, and tried to imagine the sort of life Arafat would have led in his last year and how he must have felt. Several of Arafat's ministers were rushing past me on their way through the camouflaged entrance and into the dark, cavernous structure.

A few months before he died, Arafat had called a friend of mine who served on the Leadership Committee to come and meet him on a Friday, the official day off. It was a warm, sunny morning and Arafat had done the rare thing of moving out of his dimly-lit office into the open air. He sat there without his headdress or jacket, in just his white shirt, looking small and vulnerable. My friend was touched to see this leader sunning himself, asking him what he thought could be done to save the nation. My friend said, "I looked at Arafat and saw an old man sitting in the sun, his head bare, asking in the simplest manner the biggest question of all. As you know, I've always been critical of his style of leadership, but seeing him like this, with a few wisps of gray hair on his head, sitting on a low chair in the sun, he reminded me of my own father. I couldn't help but feel sorry for him."

As I stood before the partially wrecked building, watching well-dressed public figures hurrying by, their mobile phones fixed to their ears, this image of an old man whose every pronouncement made news that was beamed across the globe, rose before me. I was told that the busy officials were going in for consultations to discuss replacements for the various posts held by Arafat before his death.

I left the ruins and walked a few meters towards the bustling street where the original main gate of the Tegart now stood in a partially demolished wall of the fortress. From this angle, the skeletal wreck of the once-proud building looked like a carcass, not unlike the state of our nation. The front wall had completely collapsed, exposing the interior of the two floors. Standing tensely just inside the upper floor, eyeing the activities taking place below with curiosity and circumspection, was a tall, armed man in his early twenties, with dark hair, a black moustache and wide, radiant eyes. He was wearing black trousers folded halfway up to his knees and a crumpled white shirt. Perhaps the fact that he wore slippers gave me the impression that he was a resident of this place. The other guards roamed all around but he kept to his post inside the door frame, as though this ruin were his home. A few friends were standing with him but he was the only one who was armed and who did not step outside the door. I was told later that he was one of the Palestinian militants wanted by Israel who had been hiding at the Muqataa, under Arafat's protection, for a long time. I wondered what would happen to him and his colleagues now that Arafat, their protector, was gone?

As I wondered about this young man's fate, I tried to identify the places I had been familiar with at the time of direct Israeli Occupation. The November sun was shining through the few clouds that hung in the sky. The door where the anxious young man was standing, I decided, used to lead to the military courtrooms. Just inside the door was the small chamber where they kept detainees before they were allowed into court to appear before the military judge. I was witness to so many scuffles that took place in this chamber between detainees and their Israeli guards. The screams of the young Palestinians echoed in the nearby valleys. The door leading to Arafat's living quarters and office had once served as the prosecutor's offices and the court secretariat.

As I was marveling at the state to which this once-awesome building had been reduced, I saw a dog among the ruins of the second floor which was missing its front wall. He was sniffing around, probably looking for something to eat, oblivious of the crowds down below and of the danger of falling from the ledge on which he roamed.

Only when I saw the rooms where Arafat had been holed up during those last three years did I understand what it had all been about. He had kept himself in what appeared to be a hideout. The door was camouflaged by an awning, giving the impression that one was entering a sort of cave.

But of course there was no need to conceal the entrance—the Israelis knew exactly where he was living and had demolished most of the rest of the building, almost up to the very wall of his room whose entrance was hidden. How horrible it must have been to be in the building while missiles were falling close by, filling his hiding place with danger. The man must have had nerves of steel to have survived for so long. For months he refused to leave. In the early 1970s, at the beginning of his struggle in Jordan, he was known to have hidden in a cave. At seventy-five and infirm, he was ending his life in a make-believe bunker.

The milling crowds paying their condolences discussed the possible cause of Arafat's death and expressed their anger at France for not revealing the truth. No one suggested that since we had the body right here in the Muqataa, it was possible to resolve the mystery by carrying out an autopsy. We had lost the confidence to rely on ourselves rather than waste our energy by blaming our troubles on others and expecting them to do what we could do ourselves.

The guards of honor at Arafat's tomb wore white gloves. I climbed a few steps to get to the marble floor in the middle of which was the grave. Standing over it were distraught men and women, some weeping. Others were reading the *Fatiha* from the Holy Quran for the soul of their dead leader. A few stood by without any apparent emotion and just looked down at the grave. I noticed it was quite close to the site of the old prison, now leveled. There was no sign left of the place where hundreds of thousands of Palestinians had suffered long periods of incarceration, interrogation and torture. It was completely eradicated.

It should not have happened this way. There was no need for the return of Arafat to signify the suspension of the legal struggle to which I had been committed. Yet the post-Oslo struggle took place within the context and parameters that Israel had set. The heroic rhetoric was sustained with all the right slogans:

the end of the Occupation and the withdrawal of Israeli troops to the 1967 borders. But the construction of Israeli settlements on Palestinian land was only speeded up as if to win a race before the nonexistent referee called time out. Except for the occasional verbal denunciation, the Palestinian Authority remained silent, failing to effectively challenge the legal ploys used by Israel to sustain and pursue its colonial enterprise. As I looked at the physical transformation in the Tegart Building, all those contradictions of the past were being made concrete. I could see how the failed armed struggle had completely dominated our leadership's vision, taking precedence over the nonviolent resistance waged in the streets as well as in the courts by challenging Israeli legal maneuvers. Arafat had managed to turn the Compound into a symbol that exclusively celebrated the form of struggle which he had championed over his years of exile, and a place where ex-fighters took refuge. It shouldn't have been this way. It was not the one or the other, Arafat was right to hold a gun in one hand and an olive branch in the other. I was never so naive as to expect that Israel could be won over by the olive branch alone, but the gun could only ever be a means to an end. Now there was nothing left to commemorate the other struggle.

### III. June 5, 2011

Unlike in previous years, this year the forty-fourth anniversary of the Occupation passed unmarked. Life went on as normally as possible under a prolonged Occupation. On my way to work, I was driving by the newly remodeled Muqataa that now serves as the headquarters of the Palestinian Authority for its agenda of proving itself to the international community by building institutions. Of the old Tegart, only the small area which Arafat had made his hideout during the 2002 invasion of Ramallah remains. It has been turned into a museum commemorating the hardship and sacrifices of our dead leader. Now the Compound has high, imposing walls with brand-new watchtowers, built by Palestinians, yet resembling those inspired by Sir Charles Tegart. The old section where the military courts and prison used to be has been completely leveled and the new posh offices and residence of the President of the Palestinian Authority have taken its place. Between the walls and the street a grand garden with water fountains provides a separation between people and politicians for "security reasons." Palm trees with drooping heads, bought from Israel, sprout out of a colorful ground display of petunias and other blooming annuals in well-organized beds.

I slowed my car as I approached the entrance to Arafat's gleaming limestone mausoleum on the southern border of this lavish headquarters of our remodeled self-governing authority. A ceramic plaque embedded in the wall announced the distance in kilometers to Jerusalem, the city which Arafat had hoped would be the capital of the Palestinian state and where he wanted to be buried. I was startled by a police siren leading a procession of cars with blackened windows, ferrying a high Palestinian official perhaps, which zoomed by, almost knocking my car off the road. As the siren receded in the distance, I found myself thinking once again about what has happened to the Tegart compound on its hill, the site of such profound memories laden with historical significance. Was it a justifiable transformation of a dismal past into a promising future? How could that be when the heroic past of those who suffered and paid heavily remains unsung, with the site of their memories eradicated?

The question I have so often asked myself returned: should I have left Palestine when I could well imagine what was in store for us? After the Oslo Accords were signed, I annoyed my friends with gloomy prophecies. Many have ended up as realities. Should I, then, have spared myself the pain and frustration? It's a moot question, perhaps. In fact, I both stayed and left; I became an internal exile. It was the sight of this refurbished Tegart that brought this home to me.

When will this exile end? Perhaps when we, Palestinians and Israelis, living on this land, succeed in scraping away all the nonsense about the exclusive meanings we attribute to our small territory and our lives in it, and begin to live without the lies of divine rights and narrow nationalist narratives that are used to justify the designation of land for the exclusive use of members of one religious group. It will end when the land and its people are rid of illusions, when my life in Palestine ceases to be conceived as that of a *samid* (Arabic for someone who is steadfast) and becomes that of a citizen. I would be free then to come and go as I choose, without attaching layers of meaning to the simple act of leaving. I would be free to live elsewhere, if I wished, without feeling I am betraying anyone. When Palestine/Israel come to mean nothing more to their people than home, only then will my state of exile come to an end, and with it my *sumoud* (steadfastness).

Perhaps it would be possible then to leave this Tegart altogether and be satisfied with simply placing markers to indicate where there was once a prison, an Israeli court, a torture chamber, and the seat of an authority exercising self-rule under colonial occupation. All the moments of the dismal past would be marked and commemorated so that future generations would not forget how we struggled to arrive at a free life in a Middle East without borders.

# MOURID BARGHOUTI

# The Driver Mahmoud

Here we are, safely arrived in Jericho, as he
promised. I still can't believe we made it. Maybe it was luck or the
cell phones or the wiliness of the villagers and shepherds or maybe—
most likely—fate hasn't made up its mind yet to let Palestinians die
in road accidents. I think most, though, about our driver, Mahmoud.

I stand waiting for him at the hotel porch in Ramallah. He arrives
more or less on time. This is nothing unusual for Darwish Tours,
who are known for their punctuality. He leaves the taxi's engine
running, steps out into the light rain, and comes towards me.

"Mr. Barghouti?"

He picks up my small suitcase (my suitcase is always small here
because of the checkpoints) and hurriedly creates a space for it in
the trunk. It's good that he doesn't lift it up onto the roof of the
taxi along with the other luggage, and good that he's picked up the
six other passengers first so that we won't waste time searching for
their addresses among the hills and valleys of Ramallah. I take my
place in the yellow taxi and tell myself it's a good start to the day.

He sets off for Jericho without uttering a word, like someone
hiding a secret and waiting for the right moment to tell it. Clearly,
he's decided to avoid the Qalandya checkpoint. The windshield
wipers are no good at removing the imprint of the fog, which has
taken on the color of zinc, and are losing their race with the rain,

97

which is getting harder. The vehicles on the street are few, the pedestrians fewer. We leave the confines of Ramallah.

Everything appears normal until he gets a call on his cell phone. He finishes it in seconds and increases speed noticeably. After a few kilometers, he leaves the main road and enters a village that I'm seeing for the first time and whose name I don't know but am too embarrassed to ask. Its one narrow street curves, then twists and turns among the houses before we leave it once more for the paved highway.

"Good morning, everyone. My name is Mahmoud and this is today's last taxi for the bridge. Israel has informed foreign diplo-mats the attack will take place tonight or tomorrow and told them to get out of harm's way. All the bastards care about is the foreigners; we're not human. The army's on alert, the roads are closed, and there are flying checkpoints everywhere. The weather, as you can see, is bad but we'll definitely make it to the bridge, with God's help. Coffee? Pour a cup for everyone, Haj—'the great man lives to serve his people,' as they say. Please, have some coffee."

The passengers don't appear particularly upset at the news of the impending attack announced by Mahmoud. In fact, the fat passenger sitting in front of me in the middle seat comments sar-castically: "As if the film needed more action! Every day they kill us retail, and once in a while they get the urge to kill us whole-sale. Big deal! They've launched a hundred attacks before and it's done them no good. They're really stuck. Like they say, 'Stupidity is trying what's already been tried and expecting different results.' The only thing they're good at is shooting and killing. Each time they attack, go bam-bam-bam, drop bombs from airplanes, and leave. What's the point?"

"It's a farce!" says his neighbor. "When you see them invading our villages and camps, you'd think they were off to conquer China, though they could arrest any of us any time, including Yasser Arafat, or expel him from the country or imprison him or kill him, without tanks or armored vehicles or F-16s. Who'd stop them?"

He falls silent for a moment. Then he says, as though to himself, "Anyway, their project isn't going well, I can tell you. An Israeli state at our expense isn't working out for them. How do they think they're going to get away from us? Do they suppose they can kill us all? The project's dragged them into a mess, there's no end in sight, and they know that each year gets them in deeper. You're right, they're really stuck."

I, who for long years have been away from these people, from my countrymen and the details of their daily lives, cannot make light of the plans of a terrifying individual such as Sharon to invade our cities and our villages. To them, though—the inhabitants of these same cities and villages, who haven't been distanced by successive exiles—everything has become food for jokes. Is it familiarity or stoicism? Is it a confidence built up by a culture of living inside the details or a sign of the resistance they embody simply by remaining in place?

I decide to convince myself too that everything's normal. I prefer not to show my anxiety over what the engineer of the Sabra and Shatila massacres will do tomorrow or the day after, when he unleashes his tanks and massed troops—themselves armored like tanks—onto our streets. I think to myself, if only our leadership, petrified of Israel as it is, could grasp the truth of Israel's dilemma the way these passengers have.

Mahmoud produces from beneath his feet a thermos of coffee which he hands to the old man seated next to him, supplying him at the same time with a stack of small plastic cups.

As the first cup is poured, the smell of the coffee enters into a stealthy race with that of the cardamom. The cardamom wins, of course. "Lord, bring it all down on Sharon's head! Have some coffee, son, daughter. It's very hot. Give some to the lady. Please, go ahead," says the Haj.

The cup reaches me via the hand of the girl sitting in front of me in the middle seat. I take it gingerly, look at it, raise it to my lips, and take a first sip.

Now *this* is coffee. It may not be in the elegant cup that would make it some other kind of coffee, but it's a *perfectly timed* cup of coffee. People can't agree on where coffee's secret lies: opinions range from the smell, the color, the taste, the consistency, the blend, the cardamom, the roast, to the shape of the cup, and a number of other things.

For me, it's the timing. The great thing about a perfectly timed cup of coffee is that it's in your hands the instant you crave it. One of life's most exquisite moments is that in which a small luxury becomes a necessity. And someone has to present the coffee to you, because coffee is like roses: someone else has to present you with roses, you can't present them to yourself. And if you do make the coffee yourself, it's because at that moment you're on your own, with no lover or anyone else to think of, a stranger in your own home. If it's by choice, then you're paying the price of your freedom; if it's by necessity, you need to hear the doorbell ring. Its colors are also tastes and flavors—the blond and the dark, the full roast and the medium—so it acquires its different meanings from the expression on the face of the one who offers it to you and the circumstances in which they offer it.

This morning, however, Mahmoud's offer of coffee comes at the perfect time and, along with the lively rain outside, sends a joy through my veins that is at odds with the bad news.

"But no smoking, if you'd be so kind. We'll be there in an hour," says the Haj.

"What do you mean 'an hour,' Haj?" says another. "Make that two, three hours... four. You heard what the man said: we may get there and we may not."

Mahmoud smiles and corrects him confidently: "I said we *will* get there."

A boy in his early twenties, with a broad forehead, a puzzling mole on his right cheek that I can't make up my mind about, and small eyes that combine blackness and brightness; a boy confident as a new lamp, alert as a lawyer seized by a sudden idea, his voice commanding but not rough. Even in his winter clothes, he looks skinny. His expression is serious but relaxed and relaxing, assured and reassuring. Though young, he drives the car with an old hand's seemingly careless care.

Between me and the fully veiled lady on the rear seat sits a sad young man who, I tell myself, must have a story. Everyone in this world has a story, and since I hate it when anyone asks me, "What's wrong?" I don't ask him why he's sad. At a passing glance in his direction, however, I find him smiling mischievously and his eyes direct me to a strange scene. The lady is lifting the end of her veil with her left hand and holding it out in front, creating a long trunk of thick black cloth with a secret passage beneath, down which her right hand brings the cup of coffee to her lips with a careful speed that speaks of long experience. Then she lowers the cloth again, closing off the alimentary tunnel as quickly as she opened it and before anyone can catch a glimpse of what it is she's trying to conceal. I pretend not to notice, even though the scene is totally new to me: during my years abroad, I have never seen a fully veiled woman taking food or drink in public. I do, however, steal another look and catch her reopening the obligatory tunnel, inserting the cup of coffee into it with the same studied care, and taking another sip. She appears to regard the procedure as perfectly normal.

In the three middle seats are two men and a young woman, of whom all I can see are her hair, which is tied in a pony tail, and her small ears, which are without earrings. One of the men must be very short, as his *kuffiya* and the cord that keeps it in place are only just visible above the back of the seat, so that I can imagine but not see him. The other is the fat man with the cheerful air. Before offering the coffee to his nearly invisible neighbor, he says playfully to Mahmoud, "My friend's from al-Khalil. Should I give him coffee or better not risk it?"

We all laugh. Even the veiled lady laughs out loud.

If he's opened the door to jokes against people from al-Khalil, I think to myself, it'll never be shut again.

Mahmoud wants to provoke further jokes to lighten the mood and says with false innocence, "What's wrong with people from al-Khalil?"

Then he adds, imitating an Egyptian accent, "The Khalilis are great guys and al-Khalil's a real man's town, swear to God."

"Are you Khalili, Mahmoud my friend?"

"I used to be, but I got treatment."

The man from al-Khalil laughs loudly and we laugh along with him once more.

Mahmoud adds, seriously this time, "I'm from al-Am'ari camp."

"An honor. Good people."

Egyptians make jokes about Upper Egyptians, Syrians about the people of Homs, Jordanians about people from Tafileh, and Lebanese about "Abu al-'Abid"—the theme in all cases being their naïveté or empty bragging. The Palestinians make jokes about the people of al-Khalil, the point being their hard-headedness. Generally, people ask about the latest joke, but Mahmoud, in a strange departure from tradition, asks the passenger from al-Khalil what was the first joke ever made about the people of his town. The man, sunk in his seat, says, "I don't really know, but my grandfather used to tell the story of a man from al-Khalil who falls from the seventh storey and doesn't die but gets up again, sound as a bell. Someone says to him, 'Here's a hundred lira to do it again,' but the man refuses, saying, 'How can I be sure I'll land on my head next time?'"

Then Mahmoud asks, "And what's the worst? I mean the joke they really can't stand."

"When the settler Baruch Goldstein opened fire on the worshippers in the Sanctuary of Ibrahim in al-Khalil and killed twenty-nine of them, someone said a few days after the massacre, 'There would have been more casualties if Baruch hadn't fired at their heads.'"

I haven't heard the joke before, even though the massacre at the Sanctuary of Ibrahim took place in 1994. I don't laugh. There have been so many massacres that they've become material for their victims' jokes. In this uneven conflict with the Occupation, which bears the most modern weapons of the age, the unarmed Palestinian hates to be an object of pity. He arms himself with laughter and irony, even at his own expense, and by making fun of his repeated tragedies under this seemingly endless Occupation. People no longer complain to one another about the prisons, the curfews, the repeated closures and invasions. I don't know whether getting used to these atrocities is a weakness or a strength. If getting used to oppression is a sign of the slave, one confident of the justice of his cause may find in it a way of tamping down his anger and stoking the elements of a hidden strength. One sign of strength in the oppressed is the ability to mock the powerful, and an unspoken readiness to respond in time, however distant that time may be. While waiting, the oppressed exercise their senses to the full in their lust for life.

It would be a big lie to claim that the oppressed do nothing with their lives and in their lives but resist oppression.

The oppressed cling to any of life's joys that may be granted them, no matter how small. They let no opportunity for love, good cheer or the pleasures of the body or soul escape them.

The oppressed strive to fulfil desires both obscure and obvious, no matter how rarely the chances come and no matter how difficult they are to realize.

I was delighted by a truly lovely story related to me by a young poet I'd met on an earlier visit, at the Shorouk Bookstore in Ramallah. He told me how happy he'd been when the loudspeakers unexpectedly announced the Israeli army's complete closure of the town and how grateful he was in his heart to the army because the closure and the curfew would oblige the girl whom he loved, a relative of his who was visiting his family, to spend the whole night in their house without fear of reproach from her parents.

The next day, when the curfew was lifted and checkpoints open-ed, the village, of course, was delighted, while my lovesick friend was miserable.

The car climbs a slight slope and then returns to the level as it regains the paved road.

Mahmoud appears relaxed now that we're on the smooth highway. He searches among the buttons on the car's radio, switches it off, and picks up his cell phone.

"Fine. Fine. Thanks."

He reduces speed without explanation.

He looks right and left before turning off the highway, dropping down into a field next to the road, and turning back the way he came.

The comfort of the asphalt has lasted only a few minutes.

He goes another short distance and then explains things to us: "We've just avoided a flying checkpoint. Why the long face, Haj? 'The hopes of the optimist are rewarded.' 'Every knot finds someone to untie it.'"

"It's all in God's hands, my son," says the Haj.

"Are you taking us back to Ramallah? My plane leaves tonight and if I miss it I'll lose my scholarship and my whole chance of university," says the young man sitting next to me in a polite voice, as though speaking to himself, hoping to hear something reassuring.

The driver replies in a voice that is fatherly, despite their closeness in age. "I've never taken a passenger back where he came from, no matter what. I just need you to help if necessary. That's all I ask of all of you. Don't worry. Smile, Haj. Lighten up.

They want us paralyzed and terrified. They don't realize we've got used to it. And you, my friend, your plane won't go without you. I've never taken a passenger back. Put your faith in God and in me, everyone. Hopefully, everything'll be fine."

A few minutes later he leaves the fields again for an unpaved road.

I'm not familiar with these roads that Mahmoud is taking, and not just because my geographical memory has faded during the years of exile; the sad and now certain truth is that I no longer know the geography of my own land. However, the car is now traveling over open country and there's no sign of paved roads, traffic lights or human beings as far as the eye can see. It's going across fields and I don't know how this is going to get us to Jericho.

Puddles of water, stones, and wild plants, scattered through a fog that is starting gradually to lift. Everywhere you look, huge olive trees, uprooted and thrown over under the open sky like dishonored corpses. I think: these trees have been murdered and this plain is their open collective grave. With each olive tree uprooted by the Israeli bulldozers, a family tree of Palestinian peasants falls from the wall. The olive in Palestine is not just agricultural property. It is people's dignity, their news bulletin, the talk of their village guesthouses during evening gatherings, their central bank where profit and loss are reckoned, the star of their dining tables, the companion to every bite they eat. It's the identity card that doesn't need stamps or photos and whose validity doesn't expire with the death of the owner, but points to him, preserves his name, and blesses him anew with every grandchild and each season. These trees have been murdered, I think, and at the same instant, in two different places, stand a peasant with empty hands and a soldier filled with pride; in the same room of night, a Palestinian peasant stares at the ceiling and an Israeli soldier celebrates.

The fine rain continues.

The road becomes more rugged.

Our shoulders touch with each jolt.

The veiled lady presses herself more and more tightly against the door of the car; she has placed her bag between her and the young man as an extra layer of insulation, for greater peace of mind.

No one starts a conversation on any topic.

Everyone is worrying about arriving safely, without anyone appearing to be worrying about arriving safely.

This is how it always is: just as the drunken man proves his drunkenness by denying it, so people's denial of their fear proves they are scared.

Suddenly, everything stops.

Now, with the car stuck in the mud, Mahmoud turns off the engine so that the tires don't dig in deeper and complicate matters further.

We get out to see what's happened.

It seems the situation isn't serious. The problem can be fixed.

"A little push, everyone."

We gather, form a scrum at the back of the car, and push, making several attempts.

Before we succeed in freeing it, I convince myself that I'm playing an effective role in pushing the car even though I depend on the zeal of the others, which seems so clear when compared to the amount of strength that I demonstrate. The old man's keenness and the young woman's determination and enthusiasm amaze me. She is the only one to do her job with the cheerfulness of a child, encouraging us at the same time with loud cries:

"Come on, boys! Put your backs into it, boys!"

The old man, happy to have been included among the "boys," tells her, "God bless your youth, cousin!"

Mahmoud drives the car a few meters forward and stops to wait for us. We call to the lady in the veil to catch up; she has stood off to one side during the rescue operation.

The mud sticks to our clothes, our hands, our shoes. Mahmoud fetches a small jerry can of water from the trunk of the car.

"Everyone take turns now. Please, sister. Please, Haj. Please, Mister."

One by one, each of us washes our hands as he carefully measures out the water.

He offers us a piece of cloth from inside the car with which we try to wipe off the bits of mud that have stuck to our clothes and we use up a box of paper tissues drying our faces.

It's still day but it looks like evening because of the thickness of the fog in the valley. No doubt Mahmoud has 20/20 vision and no doubt his relative quiet helps him concentrate his eyesight to the utmost. Now he's whispering that he's spotted a concealed Israeli tank and that we have to wait a little to see if it'll go away.

We wait.

After a few minutes he decides the danger is past.

We continue on our way.

I think to myself, a person could cross this valley on foot; horses or mules could find their way through these rocky twists and turns; but how can an old taxi carrying seven passengers and their luggage do so, with the fog and the rain closing in and the Israeli "Defense" Force in its hideouts behind the trees? I think: this young Palestinian is trying to perform a small miracle without realizing it, is being a hero unaware that he's being a hero. He's only a hired driver, but he wants to do the job that earns him his monthly salary perfectly. Right now, he's the leader of this trip and doesn't want to let us down. We are now his nation: an old man and two women (one of whom doesn't cover her hair and face, while the other wears a full veil); a man who's short and another who's fat; a university student; and a poet who is amazed by everything he sees and doesn't want to spoil it by talking.

What would you do if you were in his place, I ask myself.

Would I be capable of leading this trip?

I am a writer—that is, I don't "do" anything. Isn't that pathetic?

Or am I just being too quick to blame myself, as I always am when things go wrong around me?

Now we're faced with a real chasm.

Mahmoud stops the engine.

"Get out, everyone. We'll have a look and see what we can do."

We get out.

And we see.

We are on the edge of a cut across the road that the rains have transformed into a huge, impromptu, mud-filled trench that the car will not be able to cross unless a Greek god from the heavens of myth, capable of changing fates, appears and gets us out of this earthly fix.

Our driver has improvized our present route through this grey valley. He has remained in control, more or less, no matter how much it has twisted and turned and narrowed, so long as it has been uninterrupted, but now it's cut, it isn't a road any more. And this long, deep trench could swallow dozens of cars.

The man from al-Khalil says, "It must be my fault. I'm unlucky by nature. I've been that way all my life. If there are a thousand cartons of milk at the supermarket, I'll pick the one that's gone bad."

I tell him about Abu Wajih, who was a ploughman in our village. Once a friend of his found him exhausted from ploughing a huge olive field and told him, "Your work will soon be done, Abu Wajih, and then you can rest."

Abu Wajih answered, "I swear to God, if the Resurrection comes and I go to paradise, I'll find no rest. If there's land to be ploughed in paradise, the Almighty will say, 'Arise, Abu Wajih, and plough it.' You think He's going to ask Abdel Halim Hafez?"

Mahmoud doesn't look worried. In fact, he looks as confident and calm as if the Greek gods were his first cousins.

In just a few minutes, a giant yellow crane appears from among the trees on the other side of the trench, glistening in the drizzle. In it are two thin, poorly dressed youths, one of whom gestures to Mahmoud to prepare for the rescue.

We are now in front of a trench similar to the one at Surda, but we're in a taxi carrying large, medium and small suitcases on its roof and seven passengers inside, and it is this car and no other that has to get us to the other side. It is this car and no other that has to take us to Jericho; there is no alternative in this remote stretch of country.

There is no way back and there are no taxis waiting on the other side of this fissure in the earth.

It occurs to Mahmoud that he ought to secure the suitcases with rope to prevent all or some of them from falling off during the rescue operation. He fetches a long rope, ties one end to the luggage rack, throws it over to the other side, tugs on it, and then repeats the procedure, helped by the sad young man who comes quickly to his assistance.

He doesn't stop tying until he's completely satisfied. He orders us to return to our seats inside the car so that the two rescuers can start their work. We sit and wait.

Mahmoud issues his instructions: "Fasten your seat belts. Don't panic. We're going for a ride on the swings!"

He laughs, to encourage us and himself.

He takes his place behind the wheel, first making sure that the doors are properly closed.

A moment of total silence envelops us all. A moment as silent as a candle burning. A moment as silent as a letter being passed under a door.

Then the rumbling begins.

Dumbstruck, I watch what's happening.

The huge arm of the crane rises gradually into space until it reaches what its drivers judge to be the correct height. Its metal joints rub and chitter against one another and from time to time it groans as they lower its long arm slowly towards us, tilting it a little to the left, then a little to the right, and finally, with extreme care, bringing it down until it is almost touching the car. Next, it takes the car in the grip of its terrible iron fingers, which wrap themselves around its body like the fingers of a hand around a pomegranate, and with careful slowness lifts it, and us, into the air. We are now between earth and sky.

The suspended blob of air in which we seven are swinging is now our place of exile from this earth. It is our disabled will and our attempt, in a mixture of courage and fear, to impose our will through wit and cunning. This bubble of air is the unyielding Occupation itself. It is the rootless roaming of the Palestinians through the air of others' countries. In the world's air we seek refuge from our earth. We sink into the upper spaces. We sink upward. The only high place I've achieved among men, Grandmother, and the only high rank I've risen to in my country is thanks to this deaf metal monster. Did you pray to the heavens so often for my elevation that they decided to answer your prayers like this and mock us both? I want my high standing to be brought low, Grandmother. I want to descend from this regal elevation and touch the mud and dust once more so that I can be an ordinary traveler again.

*Excerpted from: Mourid Barghouti,* I Was Born There, I Was Born Here *(London: Bloomsbury, 2011). Reprinted with permission.*

# REMA HAMMAMI

# Home and Exile
# in East Jerusalem

## Sheikh Jarrah

For more than twenty years I've lived on a small
stretch of the Nablus Road in Sheikh Jarrah, making the neighborhood my most constant home. I moved in a penniless graduate
student in the late 1980s and found an apartment in a nondescript
mid-century building that I shared with a series of grad students
and solidarity workers who were as poorly dressed and penniless as
I was. Recklessly, I had chosen Gaza as the place to do my fieldwork
in anthropology, a year after it had exploded in the first uprising's
fog of tear gas and black tire smoke. The only way I could make it
through a week of Gaza's heavy mix of Intifada violence and social
repression was by knowing that on my horizon were a few days in
the little apartment on the Nablus Road where I could grab some
oxygen, a few sips of Gold Star beer, and remember what it was like
to have bare arms. Sheikh Jarrah was a haven, but a rather odd one.

A neighborhood of Arab East Jerusalem, Sheikh Jarrah ambles
over two hills cut in the middle by a *wadi* with its three main quarters determined by this topography. The quarter on its southern
hill is home to the American Colony Hotel and the mosque and
tomb of the eponymous Sheikh Jarrah. In the *wadi* are the mythical
tomb of Simon the Just (actually the resting place of Julia Sabine, a

111

Roman woman) and the now infamous settler takeovers of Palestinian refugee family homes. My quarter, on the northern hill (sometimes called "upper Sheikh Jarrah"), is home to turn-of-the-century family mansions that mirror those lost to Israel when it took the western part of the city in 1948, as well as to a handful of foreign consulates that survived Israel's arrival on this side of town in 1967.

## 1989

When I arrived, the upper quarter still possessed an aura of gentility that Palestinians of a certain generation continue to associate with the whole neighborhood. Up the road were two grand missionary-style hospitals: The French Hospital and the more famous St. John's Ophthalmic Hospital to whose doors I regularly delivered Hajjis, women from Gaza losing their sight to diabetes and years of hypertension. There was also the closest thing to a high-rise building in East Jerusalem: the Ambassador Hotel, whose coral-colored dining room held the only childhood memories that connected me to the neighborhood.

And there were three schools: the Mamuniyya Girls School (that Jerusalemites still called by its pre-'67 name, the Sakakini); the New Rowda Girls School (still "New" although established in 1948); and the British School of Archaeology (not actually a center of learning, but more a "school of thought"). Weaving it all together was the Nablus Road, the bustling main commuter artery in the West Bank that carried passengers back and forth through the neighborhood on their way between Jerusalem's Damascus Gate and anywhere they needed to go as far as Jenin and back. Running along its western edge was a long strip of wasteland, the symbolic remains of "no man's land" that created a narrow but comforting separation from the inexorable spread of our unwanted West Jerusalem neighbor–occupiers.

But despite all its grand offerings and traffic the neighborhood was sleepy. Or, more exactly, it was in a paralysis that began when Israel stopped the clock in 1967. New buildings were totally absent. Looking around, you could make out an odd assortment of weathered concrete skeletons protruding from buildings: unfinished projects that had waited despondently for twenty years for an elusive Israeli building permit. My apartment was surrounded by the largest frozen project—the rubble of a huge chunk of hill everyone referred to as "the cemetery," that my landlord's father had scraped out for a planned hotel just before Israel arrived. Only later did I learn the real source of the nickname: after years of battling in the courts, the father had been struck by a fatal heart attack the moment he learned the Israeli municipality had condemned his dream hotel to remain a permanent pile of rubble.

Most of the residents of the quarter were also surviving remnants of a more genteel past. My immediate neighbors were assorted versions of Palestinian Miss Havishams: spinsters and widows from Jerusalem's "good" families who had been left behind when other family members passed away or moved on to more promising futures. Alone in their grand family homes, they busied themselves by spying on the limited action offered by the street and oppressing the various helpers tasked with assisting them in the upkeep of the family shrine. And, like any good shrine, their homes were thick with icons and offerings. Each interior, like an overstocked souvenir shop, was sagging with generations of knick-knacks, fading color photos of successful family members at the Eiffel Tower or Disney World, and masses of heavy furniture served up with generous dollops of lace doilies. It struck me that as long as these old ladies rattled around these over-stuffed rooms wielding their feather dusters and frying garlic for today's lunch, family members at the far corners of the universe could live in the certainty that their ancestral city was still a breathing part of their being.

Above me lived Mary—in her eighties, with red-hennaed hair and the smoking habits of Colette. She had spent most of her adult life working at the French Consulate and, in retirement, now hosted a steady stream of visitors from across the West Bank seeking her clairvoyant readings of their coffee grounds. Next door was "Midget Lady" and her tall humorless sister. Midget Lady was a streak of lightning—always out on the front verandah, looking for company, waving at passers-by, and offering homemade *ma'moul* cookies to strangers and workmen. Because of this wanton behavior, fairly credible rumors had gone around the neighborhood that she was having an affair with a bus driver who plied the route in front of her house. Next to them was Sitt Usra, a retired UNRWA school teacher, and her slightly retarded brother. She was young and spry at around sixty-five; he was slow and old at fifty. You could walk the whole length of the road and not find a nuclear family and definitely not come upon a neighborhood child. In fact, the only men or children around were outsiders who came to the quarter a few hours a day for two of its main services: refreshment and education.

There is still only one little corner store on my stretch of road, run by Abu Ramon, originally from Rafidia outside Nablus. His unmarked shop half-heartedly offered the usual basics of cheap detergent and canned goods. But the pretence at being a regular grocer was so transparent that the sardines and soap could only have been a gesture to the neighborhood. The shop was actually a liquor store—a specialty liquor store that catered to furtive drinking from brown paper bags on the sidewalk. It was not the place you went to for quality or quantity. Abu Ramon's best were airplane-size bottles of Johnny Walker Red, but his main sellers were half bottles of cheap local brandy and *arrack* that stood in regimented rows under the protection of a small poster of St. George slaying the dragon. Luckily, given these specialties, the small skid row this begat on the pavement was composed mainly of old men from down in the *wadi* who tended to be morose silent drinkers. Down the way at Mr. Automatic, cold beer had attracted a more muscular crowd of Palestinian workers coming back from Israel, who sometimes got into brawls in between relieving themselves against the walls of the New Rowda School. That upper Sheikh Jarrah was the only place outside the Old City's Christian quarter where you could buy booze in East Jerusalem wasn't a sign of liberalism but of aloofness compensating for lack of backbone. Once the sons of the quarter had disappeared into exile, the only protection left for the remaining residents was to close their shutters and feign indifference to illicit goings-on at their doorstep.

As I was weeding my patch of front garden one day, a nervous young man with the telltale signs of stone dust on his shirt ran down the steps from the street. Wordlessly he leaned forward and thrust a balled-up *kuffiya* into my hands before walking off. The ethic of the First Intifada was so powerful that I immediately knew what to do and hid it in the house, just in time to see an army patrol pass by my front window.

The city was galvanized. Trips downtown regularly involved skirting around stone barricades and lit tires. The main militants in our neighborhood were the schoolgirls from the New Rowda down in the *wadi*, who regularly blocked the main road with the garbage dumpster and broke into choruses of nationalist chants. Walking to town one day, passing through their sea of blue uniforms, I suddenly saw the soldiers plunk one of the girls into the back of their jeep. She was a tiny thing, perhaps eight or nine, in a pea-green home-knit sweater, and was crying hysterically. I looked around, hoping to find a teacher or just about any capable adult to take on the duty at hand. But it was no use. I sucked in my breath and marched up to the middle-aged soldier wanly picking his teeth in the front of the jeep, putting on my best Miss Jean Brodie imitation:

"Excuse me, excuse me, can't you see she's just a frightened little girl?"

He found another piece of breakfast behind his tonsils and ignored me.

Then I tried, "Listen, you look like you have children."

That got his attention and he looked at me expectantly.

I continued, "Don't you have a little girl? You certainly look like you do."

And he slaughtered me: "Yes, I have a little girl but she doesn't throw stones."

I spent the better part of a week mumbling to myself endless variations of the correct reply that might have demolished his sick logic and freed the terrified little girl.

But, for the most part, inactivity was our quarter's main contribution to the uprising; strict observance of the infinite rounds of general strikes suited its tendency for somnolence. This suited me too. Gaza was my intifada, and I came home to Sheikh Jarrah for a breather. In fact, half of Gaza also came to my home for a breather, and my quiet apartment on Nablus Road became filled with the company of friends and their children seeking a few days of the quarter's healing kindness.

### 1992

Just after the first Gulf War, I graduated to a modest family mansion just a few houses down the road, where I still live with my husband, Alex. Once home to a family of five (and—given the servant bells wired into every room—at least one maid), it had been inhabited by one of the quarter's lonely Miss Havishams who had recently passed away. Her only son, working in Abu Dhabi, had inherited the place and wanted to get it rented cheaply and quickly. Alex and I found ourselves trying to cram our modest pile of belongings into a full-fledged family shrine. There was only one thing to do: gut the place.

Although living in million-dollar real estate, the surviving Miss Havishams were, to put it kindly, a thrifty lot. Each time I carried yet another forty-year collection of useful jam jars out to the neighborhood tip, I'd find one of them unapologetically sifting through my last haul. I'll never forget the sight of Midget Lady pulling an orange plastic urn (usually used for washing bums in lieu of toilet paper) out of the bowels of the tip and waving it triumphantly over her head. Once the dusty contents of the entire house had made their way out our front door and slowly worked their way back into the corners and crevices of our neighbors' homes, we were finally ready to celebrate.

It was New Year's Eve and no one had been to a party in years. The downside of the First Intifada was that, despite having a sense of humor, it had no sense of fun: parties, music and dancing were all banned out of respect for the suffering. Even if the principle is fine, the fact is that Palestine's intifadas tend to be endless. And given that we were in the only neighborhood where masked youth bearing axes were unlikely to show up during the third playing of *I Will Survive* (Palestine's favorite disco anthem), throwing a party actually felt like a national duty. I invited friends from everywhere and then got worried the gathering might be too small—so told them to bring anyone they knew. People I'd known for years, people that I still don't know, husbands just released from prison in Gaza, wild women from Nablus, all of Ramallah, and others from god knows where else—all showed up. Just before midnight, when we turned down the music to wait for the big moment, the doorbell rang. Everyone froze and looked anxiously towards the door. I opened it gingerly, trying to think of what to say to the police or masked men or, hopefully, the indignant sheikh that I was about to face, when I was greeted with, "*Buona Sera, c'e un disco qui?*" A group of desperate Italian tourists in search of a New Year's Eve party were hoping they'd finally found a discotheque. "Yes, yes, come in! No, don't worry, it's free." To this day, I am accosted by strangers who tell me they once attended a wonderful party at my house—always with the wistful conclusion, "When we could still get to Jerusalem."

On one side of our house was a deserted lot of land with olive trees and a single black cypress that stood next to an opening in a low stone wall. Beyond it was a massive eucalyptus tree blocking the view of the next house, a lovely old mansion surrounded by a huge garden. The whole pastoral vista on this side of the house was marred only by the occasional barking of a team of German

117

Shepherds, followed by shouts in Hebrew telling them to shut up. The empty lot had been the front garden of the Saudi Embassy until 1967; to the back stood the building, now surrounded by a high metal fence and guarded by the noisy dogs. The Israelis had confiscated it as "enemy property" and turned it into a listening station to keep tabs on the consulates in the neighborhood, but had left the front garden to fend for itself, probably in an attempt to keep a low profile. You only glimpsed the building's inhabitants twice a day when they tore in and out of their driveway at breakneck speed, just across from Abu Ramon's shop. This behavior always brought forth chuckles from Abu Ramon. "What do they think? If they go fast we won't know they're here?" What made the joke even better was his and everybody else's conviction that our keystone cops were from the Mossad. "They don't let just anyone do this work you know, it's international work spying on the consulates," I was told by Sitt Usra who seemed to think that only Israel's elite agents were good enough for the neighborhood.

The idea of the Mossad trying to avert detection by our motley crew was hilarious, but what made it a farce was that they had taken up residence in the only quarter in the whole city that was resolutely blind.

One day I finally caught the lemon thief who'd stripped the fruit off the tree whose branches dipped over our wall into the empty lot. From the window, I saw hands grasping at the remaining lemons. Marching outside, I called a terse hello and got back a cheery hello as the hands continued grabbing at the fruit. I was incensed. "Hello, can I help you?" I tried sarcastically. "No thanks, I can reach them from here." My diplomatic skills exhausted, I leaned over the wall and said, "Would you please stop taking our lemons." Without a blink, the gangly middle-aged man grabbed another two and said, "*Khalas*, that'll be enough." He walked over and introduced himself as Adel, our neighbor from the house across the empty lot. He wasn't the owner, but a live-in guard hired to keep a presence in the house by the owners who'd all lost their right to Jerusalem residency.

118

Unmarried and with the unkempt look of ageing bachelors, he made sure to tell me that he came from an illustrious family and worked (also as a guard) for Feisal Husseini, the noted Jerusalem nationalist leader, before bumming a cigarette off me and hauling away half our lemons. Whenever I was in the garden, I could expect him to show up, discuss the latest political situation, and cadge whatever was available: a bent trowel, a beer or a seedling of whatever I was planting. One day he asked for another of the flower seedlings I'd given him.

"You mean the tobacco plant?"

He gave me a sly grin. "If that's what you want to call it. I dried some of the leaves and smoked it—boy, did my head spin!"

In the spring, when the lot was overgrown with wild wheat, two old women from the Shuafat refugee camp would come and harvest it by hand to feed the sheep they kept at home. In the autumn, landless peasant women from the village of Kharbatha appeared to harvest the olives. Whenever the gleaners came, the Mossad's dogs would bark for the first few minutes from behind their caged enclosure and then they too would be quieted by the gently unfolding pastoral scene.

### 1993

Silence was over. The return of weddings to the two hotels in the quarter signaled that the Intifada had finally crossed the invisible line that separates petering-out from reaching a conclusion. At the Ambassador Hotel, well-heeled crowds showed up in shiny private cars to fête the happy couple to the deafening beat of Arabic pop. Across the way at its more modest sister, the Mount Scopus, West Bank buses delivered busloads of villagers to do the same, but to deafening choruses of syncopated Palestinian folk music. Either way the outcome for us was the same: every night we'd curse the happy couple as the house shuddered between the competing waves of dissonant sound systems. The Intifada may have been long and cruel, but at least it had been quiet.

But, in retrospect, the augury of the change to come was when the Israelis finally breached no man's land and built a fortress-like Border Police station just a stone's throw away from the Ambassador Hotel. By then I had so fully absorbed the neighborhood's ethic that I simply ignored it whenever I drove by. Then bulldozers arrived and started ripping up the stretches of field I had surreptitiously walked across on strike days to buy cigarettes from the enemy. Within no time the bulldozers had gouged a road the Israelis crowned "Highway One," right down the spine of no man's land. I kept using the old turn-off into our neighborhood, studiously eluding the new master of all roads. Then they blocked the old turn-off and I was forced to take Highway One. Soon enough it was announced that we had a peace process and they proceeded to make our main road, the Nablus Road, a one-way street.

## 1994

Ask anyone who lived through the early peace process years and they will tell you it was like being thrust blindfolded onto a roller coaster. After years of strike day-imposed inertia, we were suddenly plunged into relentless activity that left no time to contemplate the direction we were being hurled towards. I kept my head down, finally finished my dissertation, and got a job at Birzeit University. My long drives to Gaza were now replaced with a shorter commute where every day I could see the confusing signs of the times whizzing by. One day I'd be in Ramallah cheering as the last Israeli soldiers retreated, under a hail of stones, from the main police station; then, driving home, I'd notice another hilltop being scraped away next to one of the settlements, readying it for "natural growth." Our "terrorists" suddenly became policemen and cavorted with the IDF in joint patrols. The temporary checkpoint

Israel set up on the way into Jerusalem was starting to look permanent, but there were Arafat and Rabin shaking hands on television. Nothing was comprehensible but there was no time to think about it—unless you were a denizen of our quarter. Abu Ramon was the first naysayer: "*Khalas*, they sold us out. Those guys from Tunis—a bunch of thieves," as he read the details of the agreement in *al Quds* newspaper. Sitt Usra went even further and, only weeks into the peace process, raised the first-ever legal case against the fledgling Palestinian Authority when she discovered its policemen lodging at her winter home in Jericho in the absence of barracks. This made them vandals and thieves. Having lived through the nastiness of Gaza's long slide into internal violence, I was more sanguine: the peace process was risky, full of holes, but was still a work in progress.

But while Gaza and Ramallah were charging through the dizzying changes that constituted "state building," Sheikh Jarrah, along with the rest of East Jerusalem, had been left as an afterthought in the peace agreement. Even worse, Israel had dumped us, along with settlements and refugees, into the off-limits bin of the negotiations. While never the center of militant action, East Jerusalem—as the only venue in the Occupied Territories where Israel allowed public gatherings—had long been the center of political activity. We'd always had a constant stream of visitors from across the West Bank and Gaza stopping by after attending a conference at the National Palace Hotel or the endless calendar of women's, prisoners', or children's day events at the Hakawati National Theatre. Everything in Jerusalem had been classed as "national" as opposed to the rest of the country where nothing rated above local. But now we found ourselves being demoted by these upstart backwaters where "the peace" was happening. In Jerusalem, even the Occupation was slowly turning into a local event.

Still, at first we got a few morsels. Work commenced down in the *wadi* on foundations for two new hotels—the first Palestinian building projects allowed in the neighborhood in nearly thirty years. Up the street, a new research center on Jerusalem moved in, which gave me the chance to enjoy lunches with friends from Ramallah who were staffing it, at the slew of restaurants that suddenly opened up just down the road from Mr. Automatic. And, after years of claiming I was going to the American Colony Hotel so as to cajole terrified Israeli taxi drivers into entering our menacing neighborhood, I could now announce my true destination, get dropped at my doorstep, and even get a hearty *Shalom* thrown in. One day, as I walked into Abu Ramon's, I found Israelis dressed in t-shirts and shorts buying *labaneh*, our yogurt cheese. "*Akhsan leben ya Abu Simone!*" one of them crowed in a thick Hebrew accent. I was horrified. As soon as they left the shop, Abu Ramon leaned towards me, lowered his voice and, in a conspiratorial tone, whispered, "Those are our neighbors." I looked at him blankly, vaguely surmising that he was on the peace bandwagon too. Then he clarified, "It's the Mossad!"

The sudden friendliness of our enemies made me uneasy. Not because we weren't ready for it, but because their actions assumed our friendship could be had at the bargain rate of nice words and smiling handshakes. One day, a well-dressed old man came to our door looking for Abu Ibrahim, our landlord's long-deceased father. The elderly man was living in Jordan where a peace treaty with Israel had just been signed to great Israeli fanfare. Allowed to visit Jerusalem for the first time since 1967, he had come to see his family home, the building they had rented to the Saudi Consulate, now occupied by the Mossad. We walked up the driveway across from Abu Ramon's to the big metal gates at the entrance. He looked nervous as I rang the speaker bell. A gruff voice responded in Hebrew, "Who is it?" I explained that the owner of this building was visiting from Jordan and wanted to see his home. The voice on the other end went silent and then said, "Wait a moment," before cutting out. Within minutes the whole brigade of the building was out on the second story balcony or opening windows to peer down on us. I wondered to myself what they thought they saw: two threatening apparitions, two pathetic exiles or just an old man and a woman in jeans. Having been through this before when I visited my family's home in Jaffa, I sensed the anxiety that bordered on panic in my exiled neighbor, and gently patted his shoulder. He gave me a pale smile but his eyes kept scanning the building hungrily. Then the speakerphone came on and delivered the curt reply, "It's not possible," before shutting off.

## 1996

Friendship continued to evolve along the same path. We came home from holiday and an Israeli flag was flying from the roof of a house in the *wadi*—the first settler takeover in the heart of the neighborhood. Going in or out of our front gate you couldn't miss the flag waving at you like a bully. In quick succession three massive Israeli hotels sprouted up on no man's land. The two Palestinian hotel sites in the *wadi* languished as two pits slowly filling up with sewage and garbage. The stream of friends visiting from Gaza dwindled to a small handful that had enough connections to get a permit. For the most part, friends from the West Bank could still visit if they had the will and tenacity to put up with whatever random treatment they received at the now-permanent checkpoint on the way in. National events were no longer held in Jerusalem because, for the most part, the only people able to attend them were people like us: Jerusalem's now-demoted local residents. Soon enough the music of the competing weddings in the quarter began to fade until we finally found ourselves living in a silence that felt bereft.

One morning, still in pajamas, I went to answer the door, cursing under my breath at the imbecile who kept insistently ringing the bell so early. I found an unbelievable sight waiting outside: heavily armed police and soldiers were amassed all over the garden, up the front path, with even more of them spilling onto the street. I unlocked the outer glass door nervously and found myself face

123

to face with a bald but lithe police officer holding a document in his hand, who barked at me in Hebrew. I replied in English that I didn't understand.

"Zees is house of Said Hindiyeh?"

"Yes, but he is deceased and we are only renting the place."

He didn't understand and continued reading from the document.

"You must pay 83,000 shekel to (unintelligible something in Hebrew) for hospital for Suham Hindiyeh."

The armed men in the garden kept looking around, holding their weapons taut as if they were expecting an ambush.

"If you not pay, we seize the things of the house."

I looked past him and realized that the soldiers were guarding a large truck. Slowly the scenario became clear: they'd brought the truck to haul off the house's contents unless the ghost of our landlord's father suddenly appeared and paid off the long overdue hospital bill of his similarly deceased wife.

In a tone and pace reserved for imbeciles, I pointed out these minor hitches in Bald Head's operational plans.

Bald Head looked perplexed, turned and mumbled to one of his armed companions who, in turn, shrugged and muttered something back. When all else fails, Israeli security personnel always fall back on the same trump card and he demanded my identity card. Handing it to him, I asked whether this was how they showed up to collect medical bills in West Jerusalem.

### 1997

"Alex! Rema! Alex! Rema!" It was our neighbor, Adel, shouting over the garden wall with an urgency in his voice that said something was terribly wrong. "Settlers! Settlers are breaking into the house!" He was trembling and kept looking back over his shoulder. I looked across the empty lot and could see a stream of people, including soldiers and police, moving back and forth under the trees that shaded his house. "Do something! Call someone!" Alex called the closest thing there is to a Palestinian 911: Lea Tsemel, the Israeli human rights lawyer. I made Adel a coffee and within half an hour the garden was full of reporters as the street filled up with more soldiers and police. Adel sat in silence, with the stricken look of someone who'd just witnessed a murder. Lea turned up: "It's a test case. There are Palestinian owners but they only have West Bank identity cards. The right wing wants to see if it can make Jerusalemites into absentees even if they live only a few miles outside the city. That way they can take over so many more properties." I should have known by now: in East Jerusalem a bad incident always came with grand ambitions and a master plan.

The Israeli courts, in their usual even-handedness, ruled that while the case was being heard, Adel could stay in the house, but settlers had the right to post guards in the garden. Unable to have visitors at the house, he'd trundle over to our garden wall and speak in whispers even though the guards were well beyond earshot. "I haven't slept in months. First I was worried they would try and kill me. Every time I heard a sound I'd stand by the door with an iron pipe. It turns out they aren't settlers themselves but from a security company—these ones are Russians. They act nice enough, but who knows? Now they play loud music at night and you should see how they drink!" But there was a vague melancholy in the way Adel delivered this last bit of information and I realized that since the attempted takeover, he always politely declined my offer of a beer.

### 1999

The case went on for two years and was finally decided by politics: a few family members with rights to the house had US citizenship. Apparently, allowing the plunder of US nationals' property exceeded even the limits of American largesse to Israel. Adel, now with the well-earned stripes of a national hero, stopped by the garden wall with his new sidekick: a yappy little brown terrier called Max.

"Interesting name," I said.

Adel looked uncomfortable and then cleared his throat:

"Remember the big snow last winter? You know, the really big one? Well, it was late at night and suddenly I hear banging on the door and they're shouting, 'Let us in! Let us in!' *Haram*, there were two of them and the snow collapsed their tent. They were freezing."

"Adel, you let the guards into the house?"

"Only that one time. What's a person to do—let someone freeze to death?"

I know what I wanted to say but kept my mouth shut.

He went on, "You know, they're not all the same, the Jews. One of the guards, Max, I swear to God he's *maskiin*, just like us. He's Iraqi, well, I mean his parents were from Baghdad, the Jews tricked them into coming here. There they had a big house and servants and everything and here what was he—a guard! He had no choice, it's the only work he could find. He doesn't believe in Israel and settlers and all that crap but he has a family to feed."

It was hard to keep a straight face in light of this doggie twist to the Stockholm Syndrome.

"Adel, would you like a beer?"

He looked down at the terrier. "*Yalla*, Max, time for a drink?"

It was around this time that the Miss Havisham die-off began. First to go was Mary and then, a few months later, Midget Lady. Death then skipped a house and took Um Hisham who lived above us. Each time one of them died the quarter seemed to lose a little more of its memory. Their homes, now absent a shrine-keeper, would be summarily stripped, renovated and rented out as offices to anonymous foreign agencies and NGOs that came to promote the amnesia of "peace." Family members not living in the city believed installing an international agency—besides providing more lucrative rents—was the best way to protect their inheritance from

126

Israeli takeover. But the loss of the shrines and the shrine-keepers and their takeover by outsiders felt just like forced evictions. A friend from the neighborhood took to calling them "settlers," because once a home fell into their hands, it would never again revert to Palestinian occupants.

One morning, I saw Sitt Usra on the street, standing over a blacksmith doing some welding at her front door. I walked up and found her looking haggard and still in her nightgown, then realized the entrance was a mess of broken glass and black soot. Shaking her head, she explained that a Molotov cocktail had been hurled at the house in the middle of the night. "I heard the crash of the bottle and woke up to find the front door on fire. Thank God we had the fire extinguisher." Her brother weighed in, "We called the police and they showed up five hours later." Then Sitt Usra looked at me in total incomprehension: "They kept saying, 'You must have enemies. Who are your enemies?'" The blacksmith shut off the torch and let out a mumbled curse. If the Israeli police hadn't been so obscene we might have laughed at their absurdity and self-delusion. Everyone knew who the enemies were, and only in an instant of terrified desperation had Sitt Usra momentarily forgotten this and inadvertently sought help from their quarters.

Following the incident, Sitt Usra and her brother bunkered themselves behind a new steel door and shutters. She even had the blacksmith cover the small arched window above the front door. I'd always had to avoid peeping into their living room through the open door when I walked up the street. Now, with all the light blocked out, I could barely see them even when I was inside. Once the caretaker of all the ladies in the neighborhood, Usra was now the last of them and I couldn't help feeling this was why she'd been attacked. Because once the shrine-keepers had gone and the foreign agencies moved in, I realized that they had been the keepers not just of their own homes, but of the entire quarter.

**2000**

In early 2000, a suspicious innovation appeared on our street: a row of six neatly signposted handicapped parking spots. We barely had pavements, rarely had garbage pick-up, and our street lamps never had working bulbs. Full military escort for the delivery of medical bills or the despatch of helpful policemen to treat pensioners for their Molotov cocktail habit was the type of city service we were used to. So this sudden appearance of municipal civility was downright ominous—especially since there were no disabled people in this part of the quarter in need of a parking space. And they were placed on a vacant portion of the road, sided by two empty plots that overlooked the homes in the *wadi* below.

A few weeks later, as I passed the shiny signs on my way home, I realized that the skull-capped man standing next to the car in one of these handicapped spots was none other than the Israeli settler leader (and then Knesset member), Benny Alon—a man whose name in the press was regularly accompanied by the word "virulent." I parked and watched him from my rear-view mirror. He was talking on a mobile phone and looking down into the *wadi*.

By early spring, the first house that the settlers had taken over in the *wadi* (not far below the parking spots) had a series of new additions: an adjacent building had been taken over, its Palestinian residents evicted, and settler families, wielding babies, prams and submachine guns, had moved in, along with more gun-wielding security guards to be posted on their roofs. The owners of the handicapped parking spaces had arrived.

In May, I came home and the neighborhood was overrun by a massive settler festival. It was LagBa Omer, a day every year when Sephardi Jewish families would make their way over from their neighborhood, cross no man's land, and visit the tomb of the alleged Simon in our *wadi* when they couldn't make it to the real Simon's tomb in the Galilee. But while throngs of these dark-clad religious families regularly showed up, they were, on the whole, quiet and respectful visitors. This year everything had changed: Benny Alon and company had brought a menacing mass of gun-toting, baby-carrying, "Kahane Lives!" t-shirt-wearing settlers to dance to the horrendous din of settler rock-and-roll. The municipality had granted them a license to set up this mass celebration of violence and power right in the midst of the homes of the Palestinians they wanted to erase from their neighborhood. And they had granted their sound system infinite decibel levels to ensure that the entire Arab part of the city couldn't miss the event's screaming message. I could have screamed as much as I wanted because their noise eradicated all other capacity for sound. Thankfully, spared an understanding of Hebrew, at least I missed the specific wording of calls for my neighborhood's ethnic cleansing.

June, and we were awoken in the middle of the night by what sounded like the roars of football hooligans. Peeking out of the window, we saw a group of about forty young Israeli men—settler youngsters going by their get-up—dancing around the middle of our road with Israeli flags, whooping, roaring, and breaking into menacing chants intended to let us know who owned the street.

"It must be Jerusalem Day," I grumbled. Alex started laughing.

"Alex, get away from the window! What's so funny?"

"Look at these bullies: they only come here in the dark and with an army jeep for protection!"

October came and Ariel Sharon was given permission by the Israeli government to enter the Haram al-Sharif. We all know what happened next.


## 2002

On my way to buy vegetables from The Garden of Eden up the road in Beit Hanina, I was startled by a massive sonic boom. I jammed on the brakes just in time to see an immense cloud of smoke explode over the Ramallah skyline: it was an F-16 fighter jet bombing the headquarters of the Palestinian Authority. A few nights later, at a dinner party around the corner from our house, a joke was suddenly interrupted by the rat-tat-tatting of helicopter gunfire far over the horizon. We got up from the table and watched in shamed horror the deadly display of red streaks piercing the night sky over Beit Jala.

In Jerusalem, after the IDF provided the first bloody event (killing seven demonstrators on the grounds of al-Aqsa mosque) that gave the uprising its name, we were soon thrust into the wretched role of spectators. The original checkpoints that had barred our friends and families from entering the city now seemed to demarcate the line between Israel's brutal theater of war on the other side and the farcical normality they viciously enforced in East Jerusalem.

But the images of what was happening beyond the checkpoint were now a constant gruesome backdrop to our daily lives. "Baba, enough. Turn it off," I found Abu Ramon's son beseeching him in the shop one day. Like every shopkeeper in the city, Abu Ramon had mounted a TV on the wall permanently tuned to al Jazeera, and had been in an adrenalin-dazed Intifada thrall ever since. "You should have seen his blood pressure last night," moaned Ramon. With eyes still glued to the screen, his father handed back my change, gave me a polite glance with a quick, "God bless your morning," before returning to Nablus and the invading tanks.

As with many others in the city, however, the main ingredients of my life were on the other side—in the theater of war. To get there and back meant navigating through not just one checkpoint, but a dense thicket of them. My commute to work now involved crossing four of them each way—each with its own random moods, ludicrous demands, and particular expertise in sadism. One would be a white-knuckled traffic jam battle, the next a mind-numbing asphyxiating wait, the third a vigorous two-kilometer, rubble-strewn hike. I'd arrive at the university just in time to compare the harrowing commutes of my students who'd made it to campus before we'd drag ourselves off for the checkpoint decathlon home.

The Second Intifada was as if the relentless pace of the "peace process" had been harnessed to the four horses of the apocalypse. Life was made a pitiless odyssey through the brutish maze they had made of the landscape, punctuated by spasms of military invasion and aerial bombing. Against this annihilation of our familiar links between time, place and matter, like everyone else, I doggedly made the journey, believing I could defy the physics of despair. Until one day when, at the first checkpoint, I finally broke down. I couldn't do it anymore. I just couldn't go on. My hands slowly steered the car to the side of the road and I sat as if in shock, trying to comprehend what had just happened. *Khalas*, I would go home. No more fighting this hopeless battle. But what was there at home? It had become the cave where I hid from the horrible world outside. And it was lonely. My friends, once close by, had at some imperceptible point begun to inhabit another country just a few miles down this miserable road. Jerusalem and my home had been made strangers to them. I had been fighting the fact of their exile, and of my own. And today, I just couldn't keep up the fight.

I turned down a side road and headed home. As I pulled into my street, I suddenly realized that a flying checkpoint had been thrown down just below my house. Before the soldier manning it even had a chance to open his mouth, my window was rolled down and I was screaming at him that this was *my home right here.* Taken aback, he waved me away and I slammed my car a few meters forward into the space in front of my entrance. I got out and slammed the car door shut. Opened the front gate and slammed it shut. Then, just as I was about to open the front door in anticipation of slamming it too, I noticed a figure cowering in the corner of the garden against the wall that blocks the view of the main street. I recognized her. She was one of the peasant women from Kharbatha who used to come and harvest the olives from the empty lot. She was covered in the October dust and leaves of olive picking, and looked a thousand years older than when I'd last seen her and a thousand times more exhausted than I was. It had taken her most of the day to sneak in;

after harvesting half a tree, she suddenly saw the soldiers arrive and fled in terror that they would pick her up as an "illegal infiltrator." Hiding here, hunched against the wall for hours, she'd been waiting for them to leave so she could make her way back home with her painfully small bundle of gleaned olives. She looked at me and then at the bundle. "Do you want some olives?" she offered.

### Epilogue

Adel, my neighbor, is still across the empty lot, guarding the home he lives in. In 2006, he got married and now lives with his stately wife, Fattoum, who made him give up both Max the dog and his drinking habit. In 2008, settlers tried once again to invade their house. Fattoum valiantly deterred them by threatening to set the house on fire. The case of the house is still in court.

The Mossad is still in the adjacent building, but they stopped buying *labaneh* at the start of the uprising and are down to one noisy German Shepherd.

Abu Ramon still tends to his shop in the quarter. His son, Ramon, who increasingly stands in for him, succeeded in getting him to take down the television from the wall. A small poster of George Habash now assists St. George in protecting the brandy and *arrack*.

Sitt Usra's last ten years were overwhelmed by kidney dialysis treatment. She died of heart failure in January 2011. Her brother, who had lived with her every single day of his sixty-eight years, followed her three days later. The extended family, mostly living in Germany, has thus far kept her house as a shrine.

In 2008, Muhammad and Fawzia "Um Kamil" al-Kurd were evicted from their home down in the *wadi* by settlers. Muhammad died of a heart attack eleven days later. Um Kamil continued to put up a brave fight and, for six months, held a sit-in at an empty lot near her home.

In 2009, the Ghawi and Hanoun families also lost their homes in the *wadi* to settlers. They too have continued to fight in the courts, as well as by keeping permanent vigil in a protest tent across from their homes.

These three extended families who lost their homes are part of a larger group of twenty-three refugee families resettled in Sheikh Jarrah by the United Nations before 1967. The remaining twenty are all under threat of losing their homes to settlers upon decision by the Israeli courts.

In all, the settler master plan for the neighborhood envisages evicting more than five hundred Palestinians from Sheikh Jarrah and building three hundred settler homes in their place.

The two pits that were supposed to be Palestinian hotels are still pits. The rubble cemetery of my first landlord in the neighborhood finally got a building permit. Still under construction, the four-story building has been rented for $1.5 million a year by Tony Blair in his role as representative of the Middle East Quartet. He spends four days a month here and has never met with the families losing their homes in the neighborhood, nor ever made a statement about the plight facing the Palestinians of Sheikh Jarrah or of Jerusalem.

# RANA BARAKAT

## The Right to Wait:
## Exile, Home and Return

*You have no right to know the truth now because the truth might mean the end of your right to wait. And when the critics started to argue about the absurdist identity of Godot, you did not understand what the fuss was all about. You were smarter than all the critics and even Beckett himself, for he who has waited twenty years knows Godot.*
—Mahmoud Darwish
*Journal of an Ordinary Grief*
*For the Poet/Thinker/Revolutionary*

Even though I know better, I will wait. Indeed, the right to wait was the only clear right available to me from March 7, 2010 when I was denied entry into, and deported from, Palestine. A historian whose history is under interrogation, I turn to writing this essay in a way-station between exile and home, questioning both terms and learning how to live in and with them. When the story of Palestine and its people becomes all too intimate, reflections in writing can perhaps help me understand, if not overcome, my personal exile. Thinking of home in, and exile from, Palestine while waiting in my family refuge in Chicago, I turn also to the critic, Edward Said, and the poet, Mahmoud Darwish, for insight and sustenance—a form, perhaps, of scholarship for survival. Said, reflecting on the life of the mind as an *exile*, claimed:

> An intellectual is like a shipwrecked person who learns how to live in a certain sense *with* the land, and not *on* it, not like Robinson Crusoe whose goal is to colonize his little island, but more like Marco Polo, whose sense of the marvelous never fails him, and who is always a traveler, a provisional guest, not a freeloader, conqueror or raider.[1]

Though the themes of exploration and intellectual pursuit often overlap for Said, the most striking aspect of this sentiment for me lies in the image of a shipwreck and the "sense of the marvelous"— which I read as searching for hope in despair. Exile is not necessarily something that begins and ends. While trying to work through this paradox of exile, both a solitary sentence—a shipwreck—and a communal journey, I try to come to terms with the isolation of the individual within our collective condition.

In *After the Last Sky*, Said reflects on the photographs of Palestinians by Jean Mohr and says, "Exile is a series of portraits without names, without contexts."[2] Reading the text and looking at the photographs, I also felt a strange disconnect between word and picture. I was reduced to the role of observer; Palestine and Palestinians became something to gaze at and reflect upon. This produces a rather uncomfortable feeling as I do not want the grand myth of others to become my destiny. I read Said's observations of our tragic history through my disconnected present(s).

### A World Away

Abstract, solitary and haunted by memories that for the first generation were their own, my generation had to make them our own. Nineteen forty-eight was a breaking point: our society was deliberately destroyed and for subsequent generations this catastrophe kept repeating itself. It has been repeated in

136

continuing wars, unrelenting Occupation, and in the stories of people scattered within a collective context but without a collective place to call our own. Born a world away, Chicago-to-Palestine is both a real and theoretical distance—my own experiences are as individual as any dislocated person's within a comfortable and privileged experience of displacement. Though 1948 and even 1967 occurred long before I was born, both years marked my life, as they have my entire generation. Living the present through a devastating past is not entirely unique in the age of "modernity." Living in a real present that is as much about *where* we are as it is about *who* we are not, however, is unique to those of us born in the condition of exile. Palestine was the symbol, the photographs, the posters, the long-distance telephone calls in a language that ought to be my own but was made even more foreign because it was not.

Language for me was an indication of distance. If I could penetrate the language, I could assume the identity; if I assumed the identity, I could embrace what was real in being Palestinian. Then I could finally be a part of our history, tragic though that might be. For exile, for a generation born not of the land but certainly from it, is a consequence of our tragedies but also a tragedy in and of itself. We were born of exile, but born without the claim to it. Or so I thought. And so I chose history, to tell stories and to become a part of the story.

Through his own artful and striking descriptions of Palestinians captured in still photographs across our various landscapes, Said switches between "we" and "they" while reflecting on the photographs in *After the Last Sky*. Ironically, rather than rejecting or even dissecting this schizophrenia, I understood it as a challenge. After a certain amount of academic training, I (sub)consciously decided that to complete it, I had to be "they." It was not enough to know the history, or even work to write it (in all of the complexities involved in telling stories), I had to be *on* the land—or at least the part I could reach—to finally be *of* the land. For me, this meant living in Palestine. In time I would learn that neither exile nor conditions of alienation and displacement would be cured, rather they would add new layers to what was a rich, albeit often tragic, presence.

In *Reflections on Exile*, Said explores the point where the intellectual and emotional conditions of exile attempt to reconcile. He describes an encounter in a dingy Beirut restaurant between Faiz Ahmad Faiz and Eqbal Ahmad, where the exiled Faiz recites his verse. As fellow exiles in a contemporary port of communal exile (Beirut), Said played the role of observer. "To see a poet in exile—as opposed to reading the poetry of exile—is to see exile's antinomies embodied and endured with a unique intensity." If the focus is on the poet, then this tragedy becomes human only in the form of someone living within this *condition*. In Said's view, exile can only be seen as a site of irreducible contradictions—the antinomies of living and longing for life; of breathing and longing for clean air; of writing, composing, producing and longing for the unattainable clean or completed page. The question can perhaps be posed whether this fate is an inevitable one?

If language is the only refuge for a refugee, to try to find solace or sense elsewhere is to reject this line of thinking; home is provisional, and an exile's detachment is the truth the intellectual ponders. Then exile becomes an inevitable condition for the intellectual seeking the truth. Perhaps, but for me, like my right to wait, I maintain that the search for a home is perhaps as much about the search as it is about the home. Palestine may not ever be home perhaps, but part of our struggle is to accept that, yet remain resolute in the act of searching. Maybe this contradiction is the seed of poetry's hope and the poet's struggle.

Following this reasoning, it becomes necessary to move beyond the attachment to the unobtainable, for home is a comfort commodity that in late capitalism is nothing more than an easily manipulated lie. While Said's reading of exile is informed by this tendency, he reads national belonging into this conception as a strange but constant partner to exile. Using language as the only place to seek solace, he discovers that the antinomy of dislocation is as much about claiming a location as it is about understanding the inevitability of not finding solace in the claim. Palestine, the symbol, is our homeland; Palestine, the idea, is our dream—these two are the claim of the location; Palestine, the place, is the reality of home or perhaps the impossibility of it. I live(d) in Palestine and at the same time I dreamed of a homeland, and the living and dreaming were complements and contradictions of each other. Being in Palestine, then, as much as being denied entry into Palestine, forms the space in which this apparent contradiction exists. Searching for the "unfindable" is the inherited exile of Palestine, a shared condition that must also be experienced in an individual context.

## Searching for Palestine, Refusing to be Lost

In the midst of this existential search, my precarious world came crashing down. Being told by Israeli border guards that one will be denied entry and deported is part of being Palestinian; standing in stubborn and somewhat unrealistic defiance of that order is also part of our collective being. Palestine is under colonial rule and, as such, finding reasons for such decisions or even searching for them outside this brutal colonial framework is pointless. My body was literally dragged out of the airport because the colonial power controls all ports of entry, and the space between my Palestine and my body was theirs to control. In a horrible moment that was both the culmination and the break of all real and existential journeys, I was thrust aside and forced to leave  this is also my individual tragedy, however much it may be part of our collective condition. Pontification on all this produces the antinomies of our collective/individual exile and (im)possible search for Palestine. Before this moment I had not rejected the idea of home as a lie or even a mirage, although I worked to understand the intellectual impossibilities of my theory of home and exile. Then, I was suddenly forced to face the violence of my own disconnect and imposed exile.

139

Said never lost a sense of the tragic indignity of exile. While a life of the mind is often the place we go to to find solace, if not meaning, in the inexplicable madness and tragedy, it can be a false compromise with the reality of exile. Said is right when he says that the exiles (and exile) of our time are poignantly different from earlier eras with their modern warfare, bloody imperial powers and ambitions, and the ruthlessness of modern nationalism—ours is the "age of the refugee, displaced person, [and] mass immigration." Since modernity does not leave any space for myths, as Mahmoud Darwish warned, exile in the modern sense is about colonial conquest, control and (attempted) destruction.

Mahmoud Darwish composed *Journal of an Ordinary Grief* when he was on the threshold of transiting from one form of exile into another—from internal exile in Haifa to external wanderings in Arab and European capitals. His lucid and lyric prose in the midst of this not-at-all- and all-too-ordinary situation provokes us to situate this discussion within human experience. The poet both records exile and home to challenge all of the contradictions within each notion:

> Poetry has something to say, and it has nothing to say. Poetry speaks trust, but does not announce it. This is your homeland, and the response to the conquerors enhances your love for it because any weak point in the relationship between you and it is an opening for them. They put Palestine in the pockets of their military uniforms, yet Palestine remains your homeland, be it a map, a massacre, a land or an idea. It is your homeland indeed. No dagger will convince you it belongs to them. Your acceptance of the challenge and of this prison protects you from a change of heart. Thanks to the prison warden for making you one with freedom. Thanks to the shackles for reminding your arms they cannot hug a tree.[3]

Never too far from a discussion on exile, Darwish brings us back to Palestine. Though already an internal exile labeled a "present–absent alien" by the Israeli state, in his memoir Darwish records the fate of Palestine—movement from one form of exile to another. But as he says, "the mere act of searching is proof that I refuse to get lost in my loss." To find what is lost is not to celebrate a constructed past, rather longing for home is to be human. "It did not become so beautiful merely from projection caused by deprivation... We do not long for a wasteland, but for a paradise. We long to practice our humanity in a place of our own." To practice life is to do so in a homeland. This right to living was taken away by force and the bond between Palestinians and land and home was meant to be severed; to seek this is to claim and reclaim our lives. Exile is not life but its absence, and the "need to regain... belonging to the land through his actual presence on it" is the condition of fighting exile.

### Prefacing Tragedy

As a historian with an obsession with the history of struggle and resistance, I included Palestine's poets and artists and their work in the material I taught to give the grand sense of our tragic history. What should not have surprised me is that I learned more than I taught, for I found myself in the position of teaching *with* our poets and artists and not just teaching their work. As a student I explored home in exile; as a teacher, I discovered exile in home.

"Which is more painful, to be a refugee in someone else's country or a refugee in your own?" asks Darwish. To be a refugee within your land is to live under the draconian rule of the colonizers who stole your land, then tried to steal your life. One is never more aware of this Darwishian paradigm than when a Palestinian receives a tourist visa to travel to Palestine. We often refer to 1948 as the historical seed of this modern Palestinian tragedy but I found, rather by accident, an individual story that was the preface to this collective one. While going through old microfilms of Palestinian newspapers from the early Mandate period, I often wasted precious time reading advertisements and personal letters—I found them just as (if not more) intriguing as the straight political pieces. I noticed that a group of Palestinians in Monterrey, Mexico, wrote a note to the Jaffa-based paper, *Falastin,* pleading their case for a return to Palestine. It struck me that as early as 1928 (when I noticed the first letter of this sort), Palestinians were lingering in exile on the wrong side of the Mandate-designated borders of the state. Of course, exile or expulsion is neither new nor merely a modern historical phenomenon, but the kind of exile Palestinians have been subjected to is a direct product of twentieth century European colonial modernity. Not present in Palestine for the census conducted under British rule in 1922, these men were not counted or recorded and therefore not deemed indigenous (i.e. *Palestinian*) by the British administration. Traveling back to Palestine became a bit of a precarious journey—one that included denied entry and denied identity. Never mind that part of the British project in Palestine was to promote emigration (European Jewish emigration, as the administration fully endorsed and adopted Zionist policy as its own), the men pleading for their return confronted a new monster: belonging as defined, and denied, by the occupier. Palestinians have been waiting at borders for nearly a century now.

The story of these Palestinians was obviously a foreshadowing of what was to come in subsequent decades, and an early indication of what lies at the core of the Palestinian narrative—one must prove to oneself and to one's occupier, one's rightful place on the land. In its most simple and basic definition, an exile is someone who is prevented from returning to her/his home. Home and return, therefore, are embedded within the meaning of exile. Whether "return" or "home" are even possible are almost beside the immediate point here. Exile means being denied both by a real material power or power-structure—in our case, colonial occupiers.

Palestine was and continues to be subject to a kind of erasure unparalleled in modern history. After 1948, regardless of place or placement, all Palestinians experience exile for Palestine itself was exiled. The ship was wrecked long before many of us were born. What do we say when home is forbidden from being home? This kind of marginal existence can, as Said noted, make a fetish of exile: "to live as if everything around you were temporary and perhaps trivial is to fall prey to petulant cynicism as well as to querulous lovelessness." To be honest, the cynicism I confronted in myself and others under Occupation in Palestine should have provided a kind of immunity for the cynicism of exile outside Palestine. But what I learned is that exile within is as brutal as exile outside. I suppose it would be useful to think of the antinomy again. In order not to fall prey to cynicism, you love forever, even when you know "forever" is an unobtainable concept. You have to love with all the broken pieces of your heart, to coexist with the contradictions, not succumb to them. You live for permanence, even when you know nothing is permanent. Pop psychology says that six months is the time limit for mourning over trauma, more than that is excessive and requires medication. I wonder what more than six decades would require?

## The Ties that Bind

To be truthful, this exploration of the meaning of exile is a constant and consistent mode of self-reflection that has, in the past year, become a broken record in my head as it continues to loop and play over and over again. But this broken loop changes every time I hear it or will myself to listen.

I began this essay by saying that on March 7, 2010, I was denied entry into and deported from Palestine. That moment of pure breakdown, while all-too-ordinary for an extraordinary people, occurred after a long and arduous wait in one of the many waiting stations that mark the policed borders of Occupied Palestine. The ordinary: though I am born into my "Palestinian-ness" it is also something I have worked to understand and embrace. I may not have been born *here,* but I was born *of here.* I did not grow up *here,* but when I began contemplating the reality of being "grown-up," it was *here* that I contemplated the task of maturity. I teach in a university that is mine *here,* I live in a preface to a home that I made my own *here,* and I love with a madness (without stability and only a vague hope that it exists) that is fitting for this grand absurdity *here.* To be fair, it has been a struggle to understand the *here* in Palestine. In one (not-so-arbitrary) decision taken by a cruel and calculating colonial power, my *here* self was not only questioned, it was bruised and battered, perhaps broken. The ties that bind me to myself were all undone when an anonymous official announced in an all-too-ordinary tone that I would not be allowed to enter *here* and would subsequently be deported from *here.* Born in exile, living in exile, or returning to exile—I was not sure where to place myself. Though there are many Palestines, mine is a place, a tangible and material existence. We live a reality of Palestine that is neither myth nor dream.

But nothing fits—everything requires the suspension of the temporary. Making a life in Palestine is not a tourist trade, not a few months of experiencing Israeli Occupation, not a visit. But it is also not a settled life. The melancholy of temporary permanence is to taste its many flavors, from the bitter to the sweet. There are as many if not more Palestinians outside Palestine than those who live inside her armed borders. Palestine is a just cause, return is an inalienable right. After the signing of the doomed Oslo Accords, return took on a new form of absurdity. The newly-established Palestinian National Authority could not grant visas to Palestinians; a deal between "enemies" was signed and return was never up for discussion. The colonial power retained its ability to control all of Palestine's borders, deciding who enters and who leaves, who does not enter and who doesn't leave. Worse still, internal travel and movement within the still very much Occupied West Bank has become progressively more restricted with the proliferation of settlements, settler-only roads and zones. The division of land according to the successively absurd interim agreements have meant further divisions of Palestine and Palestinians. As life within Palestine grew more constricted, entry into Palestine also became more precarious for those of us who can even attempt entry—foreign passport required. Once in, without a colonial-issued identity card, a Palestinian has to remain as a visitor in Palestine, which essentially means living in a three-month cycle of tourist visa renewal. A job at a Palestinian institution like a university does not offer any security because it does not allow for a work permit—the Israelis do not recognize such work as work. The precariousness of life under Occupation is pervasive, and our era's brand of colonialism includes labels such as "absent," "present," "alien," "prisoner," "terrorist" and "dead"; "visitor" is thus relatively benign, but nevertheless unstable. Alien(ation) is not a new concept for Palestinians, merely an added dimension to Palestine's exile. Like others before me and others to follow, I will find a way to return. Even if return is a lie, home cannot be. Life beyond borders is as useless as it is necessary and inevitable. To think beyond attachments to home means always to think of home. Palestine seems to be the only place I can live in and with; it is the only place where I have attachments that are as fragile as they are meaningful. Our condition is not static. As precarious and fragile as it is, my life is *here* in Palestine; as broken as it is, it is *here*.

Palestine-in-exile is an idea, a love, a goal, a movement, a massacre, a march, a parade, a poem, a thesis, a novel and, yes, a commodity, as well as a people scattered, displaced, dispossessed and determined. If exile is a solitary monster, working through it and beyond it is not. If all of this is what we know, I have a right not to know it. This truth will only ruin the wait. I will wait at the borders even if I know that I need to think beyond their barriers and my arguments with words. I will linger in exile until my feet hit the soil I should know better than to worship.

Even though I know better, I will wait.

## A Temporary-Permanent Postscript

On August 25, 2011, I was "granted permission" to cross the Allenby Bridge and enter part of Palestine. Nearly eighteen months after being deported, after a legal battle that had little to do with law and everything to do with power, I approached a different border to enter the same place, full of anxieties that beset me for more than a year after March 7, 2010. Counting is a horrible pastime, and every day between March 7, 2010 and August 25, 2011—every day—I counted. As a well-rehearsed script, the Israelis also made me count hours on the "Bridge." Nine hours to be specific, each one full of fear and trepidation and an endless series of traumatic flashbacks to the deportation airport. With each passing hour and successive interview, I wondered if this was another cruel trick, if all this would ever end. I crossed over. Into what is another/same exploration. I crossed over and was "given" another temporary pass, otherwise known as a visa. I crossed into a fantastic, unsettled, precarious, alien and (im)possible existence *here* in my bittersweet homeland with/out a home and all the impossibilities of stubborn hope. Crossing was another lonely exercise in waiting, but when I crossed I found him waiting—the impossible revolutionary poet of my Palestine.

And so a new/old story begins…

# The Right to Wait

**Notes**

[1] Edward W. Said, "Intellectual Exile: Expatriates and Marginals," *Representations of the Intellectual, the 1993 Reith Lectures* (New York: Vintage Books, 1994).

[2] Edward W. Said, *After the Last Sky: Palestinian Lives* (New York: Columbia University Press, 1999).

[3] Mahmoud Darwish, *Journal of an Ordinary Grief* (tr. Ibrahim Muhawi) (New York: Archipelago, 2010).

# AT HOME IN WHAT WORLD?

A Place to Live and Curse in

Go to Gaza and eat Sayadiyeh.

As a citizen of Israel, I am forbidden from
entering Gaza.

- Sonia
Born in Tamra; living in al-Ram
Israeli Passport
Father and Mother from Tamra

إذهبي إلى غزة وتناولي الصيدية.

كمواطنة إسرائيلية فانني أمنع من الدخول إلى
غزة.

- سونيا
من مواليد طمرة و تعيش في الرام
جواز سفر إسرائيلي
الأب والأم من طمرة

# FADY JOUDAH

# Palestine that Never Was: Five Poems and an Introduction

There is something provocative about the title *Seeking Palestine* for me. It summons a journey whose destination is both real and imagined. It also conjures both beginning and presence. In either case, there is a truncation or an amputation within linear time. Four meanings of "seeking Palestine" come to my mind: (i) a Palestine that was, and then was lost; (ii) a Palestine that was, and was not lost; (iii) a Palestine that never was, and yet was lost; (iv) a Palestine that never was, and yet was not lost. One can expand on this mathematics of imagination by further differentiating the past from the present tense or mixing them together to produce other permutations. Between what is and was "real" and what is and was "imagined"; between what is and was "fiction" and what is and was "fact"; between "being" and "grammar"—Palestine.

There's a moment as a child when one asks: "Who am I?" or, turning to one's parents, "What are we?" And the answer is often multilayered, encompassing ethnicity and nationality. Once a Palestinian child encounters that question–answer, his or her life enters a seemingly endless state of suspension. Of the four meanings mentioned above, the first three gnaw at each other and at one's mind. The Palestine that was, the one "we" knew and mapped and inhabited, not subject to myth or the evolution of flags—that Palestine was lost, dispossessed, cleansed, settled, colonized and occupied; or, out of resistance, defiance and steadfastness, the loss is not acknowledged as a fait accompli and, instead, is placed in abeyance; or one accepts that Palestine never "was" in the dominant and hegemonic contemporary political understanding of being—yet what never was will not acquiesce further by accepting that it is now forever lost, and so an intense state of longing and nostalgia (for the details of life in a Palestine that never was) takes hold. These three imbricate meanings—punctuated by numbers or semicolons, pragmatism or determination, memory or forgetfulness, fidelity or betrayal—shape much of the complexity of private and collective identity for a Palestinian child who oscillates between vastness and suffocation.

For me, the fourth meaning looks past imposed definitions of "who" and "what" one is. Perhaps this fourth Palestine will help us move past the tragic and horrific limitations of the nation-state age we live in. Perhaps that Palestine that never was is true to exile as a state of being; not exile as a state of despair or eternal longing, but a state where one is free to wander the earth between the possible and the necessary return, since what has not yet arrived has not yet been lost.

## Still Life

You write your name on unstained glass
So you're either broken or seen through

When it came time for the affidavit
The panel asked how much art
Over the blood of strangers the word

Mentioned the weather and the sleepers
Under the weather all this
Was preceded by tension enzymatic
To the hills behind us and the forests ahead

Where children don't sleep
In resting tremor and shelling
The earth is a pomegranate

A helmet ochre or copper sinks
In buoyant salt water
Divers seek its womb despite its
Dura mater

And it hangs on trees like pregnant mistletoes
I'll stand next to one
And have my German lover

Remember me on a Mediterranean island
Though she would eventually wed
An Israeli once she'd realized
What she wanted from life

A mother of two
On the nose of Mount Carmel
Where my wife's father was born
driven out

My father's hands depearl
The fruit in a few minutes add a drop
Of rose water some shredded coconut
For us to gather around him

He will lead his grandchildren out transfer
Bundles of pine branches in the yard to where
His tomatoes and cucumbers grow in summer

Let them let them
Gather the dried pine needles forever he says
They will refuse to believe the fire dies

And they will listen to his first fire
On a cold night in a forest of eucalyptus trees

154

The British had planted as natural reserve
Outside Gaza

## Záhrada

From the Moorish synagogue in Prague
Next to Kafka's statue
The father wife and daughter headed to the cemetery

Death that has never been to the orthodontist
Death hiding death burying death Frankfurt Judengasse
Gates an echo nearby

They walked the streets and cubic cobblestones
The size of olive soap bars
From Nablus fascinated the child's down drawn head
She was learning to daydream without stumbling

"Look up" the father said but she kept
Her gaze on the stones they the teeth she the fairy

She will carry one back with her on the plane
Another's national treasure
The family will be greeted then asked to step aside
In a language they speak when home alone

On the bathroom mantle the stone will come to rest
Her sink is next to her mother's sink
But the father remembers it differently

The word for *garden* was it
Borrowed from another's tongue whose soldiers
And lovers were never in the galas this far north?

Or maybe from a time before the great diversions
Like *cornea* or *cave* or *earth*?

Sometimes the girl is disinterested in the cognate world
And she forgets all about the stones she's gathered
From different summers

## Mimesis

My daughter
          wouldn't hurt a spider
That had nested
Between her bicycle handles
For two weeks
She waited
Until it left of its own accord

If you tear down the web I said
It will simply know
This isn't a place to call home
And you'd get to go biking

She said that's how others
Become refugees isn't it?

## Schoolgirl

The love-rose in my heart has wilted
The love-bug

The news on the transistor
A nice man with a ponytail says

It's understandable
If you wanted to leave here for there

They were burying the evidence

Structurally

Boys in prison cells
And outside the kids play stretcher

One of them was dying
Between my hands you think

Commands injections things
To make the time pass
As hope or action

She used to chase love-bugs after school
To make them alight on her

She wanted not to have
Walked with naked men chained to a tank

In the houses she entered
A lemon an olive an apricot

### Twice a River

After studying our faces for months
My son knows to beam
Is the thing to do

He'll spend years deciphering love
The injustice or the illusion
Having been brought into this world
Volition is an afterthought

What will I tell him
About land and language and burial
Places my father doesn't speak of
Perhaps my mother knows

In the movie the dispossessed cannot return
Even when they're dead
The journalist felt

Rebuke for not having thought
It mattered or for having thought it mattered too much

Will I tell my son all nations arise after mass
Murder that I don't know

Any national anthem by heart can't sing
Take Me Out to the Ball Game?

I should turn to flowers and clouds instead
Though this has already been said well
It is night

When he gazes
Into his mother's eyes at bath time
*Qyss & Laila* she announces after a long day's work

He giggles with his shoulders not knowing
He's installing a web

In his amygdala or whichever
Places science thinks love dwells

Even love is a place? O son
Love no country and hate none
And remember crimes sometimes

Immortalize their victims
Other times the victimizer

Remember how you used to gaze at the trampoline
Leaves on their branches?

Don't believe the sound of the sea
In a seashell believe the sea

The endless trope and don't say

Much about another's language
Learn to love it

While observing silence
For the dead and the living in it

# JEAN SAID MAKDISI

## Becoming Palestinian

I am writing today from the village of Dhour el Shweire high up in the mountains of Lebanon in which, in my childhood and young adulthood, my parents, my siblings and I used to spend summer after summer, year after year, decade after decade. I have returned here to a new house with my own family after our long and terrible experiences in the Lebanese civil war. I find much comfort in this place, for it has held my life together, while my native Jerusalem, of which I have only some childhood memories, continues to be the ideal model of home, my *heimat*, where the past, present and future meet in my mind to create the one place on earth where I imagine myself resting, laying down at last the burden of anger and sorrow created in me by its loss.

I fear, however, that even if Jerusalem were restored to me, the alienated and outsider status of a lifetime will have left an indelible scar. As passionately as I believe that Jerusalem should be reclaimed by me and all those who have been, and are still being, forced out of it, I do not know what that would really mean to my life. I no longer have a home in Jerusalem; I can no longer clearly identify the places of my childhood memories. I do not know if I could ever again lay down my head on a pillow of peace and tranquility and the security of belonging in the place where my father, and

160

his fathers before him, walked. I would be a stranger in Jerusalem. By its very nature my *heimat* is unattainable, and exile, the state of not belonging, has become an essential aspect of my existence. But still, Jerusalem, my lost Paradise, regained and restored, is my ideal, the place I long for.

How is it that after all these years of separation I have remained a Palestinian in my heart, mind and soul? I am mistrustful of nationalism, too keenly aware of the ease with which it can lapse into brute chauvinism, a lesson I learned in the fratricidal fires of Lebanon. To me Palestine means the overriding injustice that occurred and continues in Palestine, not because it is unique in the annals of imperial mischief, but because it is mine, and because it is so emblematic of all the others. To embrace Palestine means to embrace all other places suffering injustice, and to proclaim one's faith in the eventual restitution of right. The paradox is that the more Palestinian one becomes, the less centered one is only on Palestine, and the more on the wider world. How can there ever be justice in Palestine if there is not elsewhere?

I have lived in Lebanon now for forty years. I cherish this place, and the place I have earned in it: I am as much at home here as it is possible for me to be anywhere. But the intimacy and warmth I established with the various places in which I have lived—Cairo in my childhood years, the United States in my student days and in my early married life, Beirut since then, Shweire always—is not the same as belonging. It is perhaps not less than belonging: in a strange sort of way it may even be more. One sees and understands so much more of a place if one enters it as an outsider. And Palestine encroaches on every perception: one views the whole world, and everything in it, through alienated Palestinian eyes, always aware of being in a state of incompletion, of an interrupted existence, of the constant need to speak up against the latest brutality and the latest lies, knowing full well that being far away makes the protest easier and less effective. Is it not true that in ancient times the worst punishment of all was not death, but banishment?

What a difference between the memory I have treasured of Jerusalem, and the memories of this small, insignificant mountain village, Shweire: Jerusalem, noble Jerusalem, *al-Quds al-Sharif,* location of epic battles and epic meanings, ancient epicenter of civilization, of present-day violence and wickedness, the "Holy Land," with its holy places—not so holy after all. But *al-Quds al-Sharif,* noble Jerusalem, is not to me merely a mythical location, a historical metaphor, but a real place, where my father was born and grew up, where my brother Edward and I were born. Our sisters were born in Cairo, with which our family's destiny was also entwined. I cherish a photograph of our grandfather, Ibrahim, who died so long ago no one can remember when, taken in the Krikorian studio in Jerusalem—a decorative signature of the latter appears at the bottom of the picture. In the picture he is sporting a heroic moustache, sitting with military bearing on an elaborately decorated horse, carrying a rifle, wearing a *hatta* and *igal,* a heavy *abaya* carelessly slung over his back. I have always wondered whether the picture was authentically "native," or deliberately posed to fulfil the fantasies of that orientalism that Edward was destined to write about so brilliantly decades later. It is strange that Daddy never talked much about his father, as he so often talked about his mother, Hanneh, for whom I was named. I wish my parents had not anglicized my name, but left me with that authentic, attached *Hanneh,* rather than the alien *Jean* that has caused me so much distress. Strangely enough, without having any idea that the other was doing this, both Edward and I wrote extensively in our respective memoirs about our English names and their significance.

During the years of the Lebanese civil war, Dhour el Shweire took a terrific beating. Several battles were fought here and many houses were destroyed. Still, after the war ended I wanted, needed, to return to it. In the midst of the massive transformations that had occurred, I needed to find something to hang on to, a place in which the past was stored, intact, in my memory and in reality. My husband and I found a battered, broken-down old house in the village and restored it, making it into a family home in which to receive our children and their families. Repair and restoration are constant elements in my life. During the war, I could not bear a torn curtain, a broken window or a hole in the wall left by shrapnel: I was constantly fixing, repairing, painting walls and shutters. I am sure this is an aspect of my Palestinian history.

Shweire is not a real *heimat* for me, only a substitute, a temporary resting place for my soul, as it is for my body, my memory and my imagination. Most of the memories I cherish are banal, quotidian ones of childhood and adolescence, but in recent years I have added memories of my children and grandchildren in this place, and thus created the continuity which the Palestinian in me craves. Beirut, in which I live more fully, is my place in reality, but I have no childhood memories there, no nostalgic recollections; though my present is immersed in it, the city is unconnected to my past.

It was Mother and her family who had, in the early days of their marriage, introduced my father to Shweire, her mother's native town. Here Mother, born and raised in Nazareth, linked up with her Lebanese cousins and maternal aunt and uncles who came every summer. Since his first time here, returning to it became an obsessive, deeply necessary summer ritual for my father, and every summer beginning in the early forties, he and Mother brought their growing family from Cairo, after spending a few weeks in Jerusalem. I remember the train rides from Cairo to Palestine, the summer weeks in the family house in Jerusalem, then the drive first to Beirut and on to Dhour el Shweire. The borders were already there, I suppose, but had not yet become the absolute and bloody barriers they are now. We used to stop in *al Khayzaran*, on the shore between Tire and Sidon, for fish. I hated fish when I was a child, and I do not remember if I was forced to eat it on these trips as I was forced to at home or whether my parents, in their fatigue, mercifully let me off what they regarded as a Protestant duty to eat whatever was presented to one and be thankful for it. After 1948, we used to fly directly from Cairo to Beirut, then drive up to Dhour el Shweire.

I always used to get sick on those flights and then especially on the long drive up the rough, winding mountain roads, exacerbated by the smell of benzine which the ancient cars exuded. This was part of the summer ritual: "Stop the car, Jean needs to throw up."

My father loved Dhour el Shweire because in it he felt free of all encumbrances. Here, unconnected, he could transcend his problematic multiple identities, the rival and stressful claims of his Palestinian/American/Egyptian histories, as well as the growing problems in Palestine and Egypt that, as time passed, caused him much distress and anxiety. He had emigrated from Jerusalem in the early years of the twentieth century and became an American citizen during World War I, when he joined the US army and fought in France. In the 1920s he returned to Jerusalem where he and his cousin, Boulos Said, his sister Nabiha's husband, started their business, the Palestine Educational Company. Eventually they expanded the business to Jaffa and then he went to Cairo, the great regional metropolis of the time, to expand it further. So every summer he came to this village to unwind, to forget and to relax.

Every morning in Dhour el Shweire he would put on comfortable, easy old clothes, changing in relief from the smart suit, starched white shirt and tie he always wore in Cairo. He would wear worn-out shoes, about which he and Mother used regularly to quarrel. "Throw them out," she would scold, "they are awful." "I love them," he would respond, stubbornly embracing their shabby comfort. An old itinerant Armenian cobbler would come by once or twice a week, calling his trade: "*Saleh lastik, saleh lastik*," and polish those old shoes. Once dressed, Daddy would pick up his walking stick and give his worn panama a smart tap as he placed it on his head. The panama emphasized his marked resemblance to Maurice Chevalier, of which he used humorously to boast, and one would half expect him to burst into song and kick up his heels in vaudeville mode as he went off, swinging his stick, into the village to buy the fruits and vegetables for the day. He always bought too much and Mother always complained when the delivery boy brought them home to her. "Where am I going to put all this?" she would cry. "Where shall I get the water to wash all this with?" There was never enough water in Dhour el Shweire with which to wash the vegetables or, for that matter, the five children who had spent the day out in the forest and the dirt, exploring, playing, collecting mud and pine needles on their clothes, and sweating in the sun.

Daddy spent his mornings, after the shopping, playing bridge, until one of us was sent to summon him home when lunch was ready. After lunch and siesta, he would venture forth again to play bridge or *tawla* in the village, or he and Mother would receive their friends or visit them for an afternoon of conversation and cheerful banter.

Even today, after all these years, whenever I walk in the village I see, as clearly as if they were alive, the ghosts of my father and mother walking arm in arm down the main street of the village, so unchanged despite the passage of time. I see my brother and sisters, when we were all young, walking around the village, hiking and bicycling the forested paths in the surrounding area, playing tennis and ping-pong, and most of all, reading. I did most of my foundational reading here in the enforced period of quiet after lunch, when my parents took their siesta. It was during the long summer months in Dhour el Shweire that our life as a family was lived most intimately and consistently. It was in the summer, when we were all on vacation, that our closeness was formed and nurtured, never to be undone.

Perhaps it was also here, where we did not really belong, where we were so emphatically temporary, summertime residents, who came and went from and to our real lives, that our feeling of being outsiders was most dramatically and permanently created. And no doubt this outsider status has been passed on to my children and grandchildren as well, for they come and go to Shweire, too.

It is terribly important to me that I remember the kinds of detail I have recorded here. Most of my life I have been collecting and storing memories, even of such mundane and unimportant quotidian details, with a kind of desperation that is part of the Palestinian imperative. Holding on to the past, clutching at it as it flies away and would otherwise fade into oblivion, embodying it and rendering it concrete in individual memories, memories of places and faces, clothes, foods and rituals. This is not a futile and damaging personal fixation; it is a politically charged community action which feeds the urge for a redeeming justice. Holding on to the past and the knowledge of what the past contains and teaches forms the basis of the exile experience for Palestinians. If we forget the images stored in our memories, we let go of the past, of a time when Palestine was an integral part of the Arab world, not cordoned off and separated from the rest with guns and barbed wire and high concrete walls, and my father's native Jerusalem, unscarred by the ugly colonies that today surround it, was an Arab city like all the others. I still think of it as such, however changed I know it is. Remembering restores my mother's rightful place in her native Galilee where her father, the pastor, taught her to identify and love the fields where Christ walked; in Safad, her father's native town, and in Nazareth, where she was born. If we forget the injustice that was done, and continues to be done, we become complicit as much in the endlessly oppressive violence as in the failed leadership of the past, and in the cowardly compromises and vague assurances offered by those who today hold power without legitimacy. We let go of our anchor and lose ourselves in the turbulent seas of modern history and its broken ideals.

Most important of all for me, clinging to the memory, the history of the injustice and writing about it and my connection with it, is the only form of resistance I can offer. And resistance is my lifeline, my only way of dealing with the excruciating realities on the ground.

In Cairo, though officially American, my father was known as a Palestinian. He was always addressed as "Khawaga William," and both his Arabic and his English were marked by what I have since learned to recognize as a clear Palestinian accent. He always used such Jerusalem words as *tatleh* for jam, *babooj* for slippers, *matakkeh* for ashtray, *bashkir* for towel; he enjoyed more than anything dipping his bread into a plate of *zayt wa zaatar* as he had done as a child in Jerusalem.

But still he often spoke of himself as an American and urged us to embrace what he believed were American values. He taught us to admire an America which he idealized to us, the America of justice and freedom and individual rights, the America in which standing up for what you believe—a moral duty for all—would inevitably lead to justice. This business of standing up was one to which his Protestant background added an extra dimension. One of his favorite books, from which he often quoted, was Ronald Bainton's biography of Martin Luther, *Here I Stand*; taking stands was perhaps the most important and lasting of our father's moral training of his children.

My father particularly admired American efficiency, inventiveness and progress, and believed that the American spirit was also one of adventure and hard work. And he believed fervently that the virtuous and fearless spirit of America would eventually lead to the redressing of the injustice done in Palestine. I can see him, and others of his generation, earnestly explaining to his European and American business associates or to our teachers or random acquaintances, the story of Palestine, pinning them down to listen to his tale, fixing them with his eye like the Ancient Mariner. He and his contemporaries held the firm belief that if only westerners could *know* the story of Palestine, they would automatically sympathize with it and would, therefore, be on our side. And not just be on our side, but act accordingly. All they had to do to win the battle for Palestine was to explain, to tell the truth, to tell what really happened. The problem, they thought, was that westerners had been deceived and had got the story wrong. The truth would set us free. I think Daddy died believing that the truth, properly explained and in good English, would set us all free.

I remember when, decades later, it suddenly dawned on me, with an awful shock, that the truth was not enough—though telling it remained an absolute and necessary duty—and that what mattered was plain brute power.

If my father so admired and believed in America, why did he not take us, his wife and five children, to live there? Why did we continue to live in Cairo? Though we all loved the great city, we were never under the illusion that we were Egyptian or could ever become Egyptian. And although we shared the Egyptian experience with imperialism, revolution and decolonization, we could not influence it directly. There was never any possibility that we could be politically involved; we were, quite simply, foreigners. The experience of exile—the state of being where you do not belong—was the first political lesson we all learned, though we may not have understood or recognized it at the time.

So why did he not take us to go and live in the US, the land of justice, freedom and opportunity and standing up for what you believe? Perhaps it was just because his business had become too embroiled with local affairs to simply cut and leave, but I think it was also because he wished to stay close to Palestine, to follow its destiny. And could it as well have had something to do with the sign he had once seen in Brooklyn, about which he told us many times: "Give a dollar to kill an Arab?" He had had a taste of the alienating anti-Arab American biases long before any of us did.

It was my father who taught us to be Palestinian, and to have political awareness. He used to scold young Palestinians for going to the cinemas in Jerusalem, chiding them for their carelessness, reminding them that the price of the tickets they had bought included a contribution to the Jewish colonial effort. I believe the idea of boycott and resistance was planted in us then, in those early days, hearing talk about how everyone, but especially Jerusalemites—who by the nature of their city were more susceptible to the danger than others—should avoid the pitfalls of carelessness and be sure not to play into the hands of the Zionists, unintentionally supporting what they should consciously be resisting.

In Cairo, many of his close friends were Palestinian and he took all his relations, especially his widowed sister Nabiha and her family, as well as Mother's family, under his wing when they came to Cairo in 1948, shocked and shattered. He saw it as his duty to hire as many Palestinians as he could in his business and to help others find employment in those places where he had some influence. He especially used to talk to me and my sisters of the young women from good Jerusalem families who were stranded, uprooted and penniless, with no particular skills, whom he hired and gradually trained as secretaries. This experience led him to believe strongly that his daughters should acquire not only diplomas but also practical skills that would allow them to survive any upheaval. But it was also for us a lesson in solidarity.

My father was always impatient with Palestinians who "whined" over their losses. "Whining," for him, as well as for my mother, was a sign of weakness, a futile exercise for which neither had any patience. I do not remember my father talking much about his own losses when the western part of Jerusalem, where his family house and his business stood, fell to the Israelis. I was too young then, and a girl at that, to inquire or to be taught, and therefore to understand, quite what had happened. Edward had better memories of the 1948 war and its consequences and knew the details of the family losses, not only because he was several years older than me, but because he was a boy. I have paid a heavy price in my political life for being female, and alienation from the political processes is certainly one of the components of my Palestinian identity.

But one great loss I remember well occurred during the upheavals that preceded the Egyptian revolution of 1952. On January 25, 1952, an irate crowd, in reaction to British atrocities in the Suez Canal zone, surged through the streets of downtown Cairo, burning everything in its path, including my father's business which was totally destroyed. My parents' gallant reaction to this catastrophe, following so closely on the loss of Jerusalem only three years earlier, was to become for me and my sisters—Edward was already away in boarding school—a great lesson in courage, morality and steadfastness. Later, Mother boasted of how, rather than weeping and bemoaning his loss as so many others did that day, my father immediately resolved to rebuild, and how he set off, as soon as it was safe to do so, to clear the debris with his own hands. During the Suez crisis my parents were advised by the American embassy in Cairo to leave the country, but they refused to abandon the city, their friends, neighbors and employees. This was another great lesson to us all, which was later to have a major impact on our lives. My decision to remain in Lebanon throughout the war, despite the dangers, was no doubt based partly on this memory, as well as on the Palestinian exodus of 1948.

I think it is ironic that our father's idealization of America, so contrary to the almost hysterical American support for Israel in recent decades, should have had such an enormous influence on us. But I have also often thought about our Christian, and more specifically, our Protestant, upbringing as an important factor in our development, especially in the construction of our attitude towards Palestine. I learned to recognize this factor early on in my own life, especially as I raised my children and helped to hone their political attitudes during their childhoods, which coincided with the Lebanese civil war. But I believe that in the huge volume of writing by and about my late brother, Edward, the Christian element of his upbringing has been neglected. This is in no way to suggest a simplistic explanation for his vastly complex personal, scholarly and political development, or to imply a religious, sectarian or fundamentalist view of the world on his or my part. We are all intensely secular in our outlook, and few members of our family, least of all Edward, became church-goers when we grew up.

As children and adolescents, however, we were compelled by our parents to attend church services every Sunday. Formal lessons in catechism preceded our confirmation in the Anglican church. The continuous presence in our lives of our beloved and very pious grandmother, who was the daughter and wife of Protestant pastors and who always said her prayers and read her Bible and urged us to do the same, had a huge, though almost ethereally gentle influence on us. So did the presence of our Aunt Nabiha who was a pillar of the Palestinian Anglican church, first in Jerusalem and then in exile and who, like Mother, always wore a hat to church, thus definitively sealing with her appearance her status as a good Protestant. The repeated readings in Sunday school from *The Book of Common Prayer*, the *King James Bible* and especially the *English Hymnal*, were reinforced at the daily morning assemblies and saying of grace at our British colonial schools. These helped form not just our intimacy with Christianity, but also our sensitivity to the English language. All this left a profound cultural impression on all of us, whether we have been ready to admit it or not.

I believe that this religious formation, combined with the political ideals my father preached to us, had much to do with the development of our attitudes towards Palestine. We nurtured a profound belief in the attainment of justice as the ultimate form of goodness, for which an uncompromising personal struggle by each individual was required; the pervasiveness of morality in all aspects of life, including politics, economics and social relations; an intense sympathy with the suffering, the wounded, the poor, the hungry, all bred not just from the practical life, but also from the repeated pronouncement in our house of the Sermon on the Mount and parables such as that of the Good Samaritan. The emphasis on turning the other cheek, with which our parents handled our frequent sibling quarrels, planted in us the strong belief that violence and revenge were forces to be rejected at all costs. The live example of our Aunt Nabiha's solidarity with the less fortunate Palestinian refugees and her selfless efforts on their behalf, also led to our absorbing the lesson of public service as a requirement of a full humanity.

All this combined later with socialist and leftist thought to produce a very particular and personal form of political ideology that emphasized a humane and almost spiritual relationship between human beings, and the rights that they should expect to share.

My background has led me to be deeply aware of the lost place of Christianity in the working out of Palestinian symbolism. This loss has had a deleterious effect on the general discourse. In the vicious propaganda of the conflict, those we confront today on all sides have tried to paint a picture of what has come to be known as "the Judeo-Christian" western world in endless and ancient conflict with the Muslim world over the "Holy Places" in the "Holy Land." Restoring Christian Palestinians to their rightful place in the public awareness of their history and political participation would immediately shatter this false equation and thus reestablish the entirely political nature of the conflict.

My parents always differentiated between religion and politics, between Judaism on the one hand and Zionism on the other. Daddy often spoke of how, as a boy in Jerusalem, he used to light the candles and oil lamps of his family's Orthodox Jewish neighbors on the Jewish Sabbath, as they were not permitted by their beliefs to do so themselves. Much to his chagrin this kind of natural relationship, recorded also by many memoirists of the period and continued in our lifetimes, was later ruined by the politics of Zionism.

Nor did my parents in any way regard being Christian as antagonistic towards Islam or Muslim culture, let alone Arab history. They felt strongly about their Arab roots and history and never indulged in minority syndrome politics or emotions. Quite the contrary. I heard my mother, who had read deeply in Arabic literature, more than once defending *sharia* from the charge of discriminating against women in the unequal distribution of inheritance. *Sharia*, she would say, saw to it that a brother received more than his sister's share of their inheritance because he was expected to look after her in the event that she never married or became widowed. I think this attitude of hers had much to do with her painful awareness of being an only sister to several brothers, all of whom had lost homes and livelihood in Palestine and were therefore unable to offer her any assistance should she have needed it. She was also always aware of her mother's penniless status and her dependence on her children, and she was terrified that she might one day suffer the same fate. Deep anxiety, I have learned, is a major aspect of the Palestinian experience.

Singing hymns and songs, which both our parents loved to do, discovering our father's huge library of classical music records, the piano and ballet lessons which we took, our regular attendance at the opera, encouraged the love of music which was so to define all our lives. It brought Edward a special kind of fame in his maturity: his love of music and literature helped form his profound belief in the humanism that refined and characterized his political attitudes.

The kind of life we lived in Cairo—a life of material comfort, family warmth, cosmopolitan outlook and wide cultural experience—was not blind or thoughtless, nor was it based in ignorance of the world. The fate of our homeless grandmother weighed heavily on our childhood—perhaps especially on the girls in the family. Aunt Nabiha's constant conversation—she had very little else to say, as I remember—was of the latest misfortune to befall one or another of the Palestinian refugee families she had taken under her wing. Also, we grew up with our parents' deep awareness, constantly articulated, of the terrible social injustices in Egypt, and with the knowledge of the huge rifts between rich and poor, so visible to us on the streets of Cairo. Still, the life of comfort and love that we lived helped create a confidence in humanity that made us believe in an ultimate and truly just solution for Palestine, where many of our more cynical contemporaries see only a future of injustice without end, brought on by the implacable enmity of the powers that be, and therefore the necessity of coming to terms with it.

The great political lessons of my childhood and adolescence in Cairo—other than Palestine, of course—were the bloodless Egyptian Revolution of 1952 and the Suez crisis of 1956. The first showed that it was possible, in the real world, to achieve political change without violence; and Suez taught me the reality of imperialism in all its viciousness, treachery and violence, as well as the necessity, and the costs, of resisting it.

My Egyptian childhood ended with Suez. I was sent to America for my undergraduate education, and then spent several years in Washington DC as a bride and young mother during the thrilling, revolutionary 1960s. I was hugely impressed by the struggles for civil rights and against the Vietnam war and later, of course, by the women's movement, with which I deeply identified. It was a marvelous time in which that idealized version of America that my father had proposed was actively becoming reality: Americans in all walks of life were taking stands against injustice, hatred, cruelty and violence. In a strange sort of way, living in the American 1960s was for me rather like going home.

But eventually the anti-Arab and anti-Palestinian stance taken by so many Americans and by the vast majority of public figures, whether in politics or the media, at first a surprising and painful nuisance, gradually became almost intolerable. The American reaction, both private and public, to the 1967 war was so unfair, so based on racial prejudice, on an abject ignorance of history, on widely expressed—and fundamentally immoral—admiration for military prowess and conquest, that it undermined my faith in the great American idealism with which I had been raised, while deeply reinforcing my Palestinian and Arab identity. It was a most disheartening time to be an Arab in America.

I became aware of the political activism of Native Americans against the great injustice they and their forebears had suffered, which bore an uncanny resemblance to the Palestinian story and which seemed to have taken that story to its logical conclusion. For the Native Americans, there could be no meaningful redress, only pretended remorse on the part of those who had taken away their land and their history, and had no real intention of restoring either. I read Dee Brown's book, *Bury My Heart at Wounded Knee*, and found it to be not only unutterably sad, but unbearably prophetic of a possible conclusion to the Palestine story. The thing was done, and it was impossible to imagine that it could be undone or even corrected.

My family and I returned to Lebanon a few years after 1967. From that time on I was to directly experience the immense violence of the Israelis: I was a child in 1948 and in America during the bravado performance of 1967. But I was in Beirut during the 1978 and 1982 invasions of Lebanon, and the atrocities of 1993 and 1996. I have been witness to the 2002 reinvasion of the West Bank, the brutal occupations of Palestine and Lebanon with their detention and torture centers, and the most recent and terrible attacks of 2006 on Lebanon and of 2008–09 on Gaza. The almost flamboyant nature of this violence, along with the daily dose of assassinations, killing of children, random arrests, bureaucratic harassment, house demolitions, misappropriation of family homes and lands, bulldozing of olive and orange orchards, and other forms of oppression has been meant, I suppose, not just to defeat, but to batter the collective spirit into total submission. Far from submitting to it, I—all of us—have felt the need to resist, not just as Palestinians or Lebanese, but as human beings.

But it was not only Israeli violence that I felt the need to resist. During the long civil war that began in 1975, violence itself, so cruelly random in selecting its victims, became for me an unacceptable medium for change, and I came to see crude nationalism as the cause of much evil. The bloody confrontations between Palestinians and Lebanese took me by surprise and caught me in a vise of deep emotional ambivalence. It was clear to me that, however committed I was to the Palestinian cause and however much I disapproved of the anti-Palestinian forces, especially those who acted in the name of a Christianity which I felt they violated, the violent division was futile and totally unnatural, and caused huge damage and misery to large numbers of people. It was a bloody, local confirmation of the pernicious Sykes-Picot agreement, until then so widely denounced: rival nationalisms and enmities were created where none existed before; members of families who used to freely move about the area were separated and split apart; tens of thousands were forced into exile, many for the second or third time. I had relatives who were totally committed Lebanese nationalists and I had other relatives who were as committed to Palestinian nationalism. My family connections were daily proof to me that the Lebanese and Palestinians were organically related, and thus the separation that had been created was doubly absurd, and doubly destructive.

Since that time, the two have become nominal friends: speeches of mutual support and respect are regularly given, but the wounds are deep and have not entirely healed. Palestinians in Lebanon, separated from their homeland and their fellow Palestinians, abandoned by a leadership that has moved on, continue to have to bear the memory of the conflict like a sack full of heavy rocks, both in their wretched camps and outside them.

But then, the story of Palestine is precisely a story of division, scattering, distance, but at the same time the will to reconnect, to re-gather, to reunite and to restore. Our exile is a community exile from the root, the source, the center, that which holds us all together. *The falcon cannot hear the falconer. Things fall apart / the center cannot hold.* We are at once the falcon and the falconer. The falcon travels far, soaring high in the sky, searching for the goal, the object of the adventure, the end of the journey; but despite the soaring grace, the circling freedom, the apparent independence, it finds security only in the controlling call of the falconer. The falconer waits with the thick leather glove on his outstretched forearm, confident that the captive, his friend, will return as soon as it is called, and the hood will once again be placed over its face, its vision no longer its own, but his to give and take. Together they form a unit, a single entity, and each owes his being to the other.

But what if the connection between them is broken? The falcon will not return: it will continue to fly in circles forever, lost in the sky, blinded by the singular vision it has gained, waiting for a call that will not come. And the falconer stands forever, feet fixed to the ground, arm outstretched, waiting for the falcon that will not return. Without each other, neither the falcon nor the falconer has any meaning.

What am I without Palestine? And what is Palestine without me?

# MISCHA HILLER

## Onions and Diamonds

On May 15, 2011, during a demonstration to mark Nakba Day on the Syrian-Israeli border, Hassan Hijazi, a Syrian citizen and the son of Palestinians expelled to Syria in 1948, made it across the border with others into the Israeli-occupied Syrian Golan. He then traveled all the way to Jaffa by hitchhiking and taking the bus. He was drawn to Jaffa because that is where his father came from. "I don't want to go back to Syria," Hijazi said once he was there, "I want to stay here in my village, where my father and grandfather were born." He then handed himself in to Israeli police.

I envy Hassan his certitude. He is, in one sense, better qualified than I to write about exile. To him it is straightforward, a matter that can be undone by physically returning to where you belong. Unlike him, I would not be so confident of wanting to settle somewhere I had never been, simply because one of my parents had been born there. But we are all, according to Gary Younge in his *Who Are We— and Should it Matter in the 21st Century?* a product of time and place, and like many Palestinians, I was born in the diaspora, taking the citizenship of the place where I happened to be born.[1] For various reasons, many, like myself, have never even been to what is left of Palestine. And now a third generation of people descended from Palestinians is growing up around the world, increasingly diluted (and indeed enriched) by time and place and, like myself and now

178

my children, by parents of different ethnicity and nationality, making once obvious loyalties weaker and a universal outlook stronger. So, does this make the first and second generation of people born to diaspora Palestinians any less Palestinian? Is it fulfilling Zionism's hope that, in time, Palestinians will give up their right to return as those who were originally displaced die and their young get on with their lives elsewhere?[2] The answer is no, but not because of some romantic notion of the pull of the homeland or some nationalistic sense of needing to be embedded in an ethnically defined nation. Not for me, anyway. Nor, I suspect, for a lot of Palestinians living relatively normal lives abroad.[3] So the question is, what is it that ties us all back to Palestine?

Human beings are not identifiable through a single aspect. We are each a cross between an onion and a diamond, multilayered and multifaceted, both difficult to peel and brilliant to behold from different angles. Increasingly multiethnic, of differing political and social shades and hues, religious beliefs and personal aspirations, we try to make sense of our place in the world. People united in one facet will most likely disagree in another, which makes for a richer, more diverse world, but can sometimes make for difficult bedfellows. Personally, I have never felt comfortable around nationalistic fervor or pride of any kind, and after living in Beirut during the civil war, religious sectarianism and tribalism have become anathema to me. I remember being in school in the late Seventies and making the mistake, in an attempt to rise above it all, of declaring myself to be non-religious. In Lebanon at that time (and perhaps even now), being a non-believer was worse than being someone from another religion, and if anything could unite different religions it was a hatred of non-believers. (On a more tragic note, people were summarily executed at roadblocks, not just for being from a different religion, but for being from *another sect of the same religion.*[4])

Nationalism and tribalism—creating deep divides often based on little more than arbitrary differences—work on the basis of exclusion, not inclusion, and assume an implicit superiority over others. Due to my mixed ethnicity, I have never felt that I fully belong in either camp, a feeling bolstered by being placed on either side of my ethnic heritage depending on the context. I'm described variously in book blurbs and reviews as Palestinian, British, Palestinian-British, British-Palestinian, Anglo-Palestinian, etc.—all clumsy labels that ghettoize more than they describe. Also, since my Arabic is not good enough to write with, I am uncomfortable with being labeled an Arab writer. But, as Kwame Anthony Appiah says in *The Ethics of Identity*, "Our identities are neither wholly scripted for us, nor wholly scripted by us." I am a British citizen by birth and I describe myself, if I have to, as being of English and Palestinian descent, which is technically accurate. I like to move between these two (or ignore them both) depending on which layer or facet of myself I am showing. In the past, I fluctuated between desperately trying to belong completely to one tribe or the other (not easy), and distancing myself from one or the other, until eventually I stopped worrying about what others thought and went with the comfortable if trite: just being me.

Does any of this matter? Not really. It makes me wary of pigeon-holing, distrustful of how people are described. What it does do, and this is invaluable for a writer, is give you a slightly displaced view of things, one that is not blinkered by whatever flag you happen to be born wearing. Being "Out of Place"—as Edward Said aptly named his memoir—is not a bad spot to inhabit. You can thrive in ways that you would not if you were a fully signed up and accepting member of the tribe. Many writers and artists have flourished in exile and many have exiled themselves precisely for this reason—think of those American writers self-exiled in Paris, Jewish writers who fled to America in the build up to the Second World War, Russians who fled from both the Tsars and the Communists, numerous contemporary Arab writers living in exile. Self-evidently, we would not have heard of these people if they had stayed at home and kept quiet. So in one sense we should embrace it, celebrate it. There is no doubt that it is liberating—being able to think against the grain—even if it is a struggle.

As writers and artists we can also tap into the incredible wealth of material Palestine presents us with: conflict, injustice, thwarted dreams, forbidden love, misplaced loyalty, clash of cultures—it is all there in abundance. They say the subject matter chooses the artist, not the other way around, and it is true that there is a particular need for Palestinian stories to be told. I found this with my first book, *Sabra Zoo*. It followed me around for years, bullying me until I got rid of it by writing it down. However, I reject completely the idea that writers who are Palestinian, or descendant from Palestinians, are duty-bound to write about Palestine or the Palestinian experience, any more than Black writers are obliged to write about the experience of being Black, or Jewish writers the experience of being Jewish. Nobody is duty-bound to write about any subject and, indeed, many a well-meaning writer has floundered by trying to be true to some political point before being true to his or her art. If writers and artists have any duty beyond aestheticism and escapism (and even this is arguable), it is to report on the human condition in a candid and compelling way. As "exiles," we are in a position not just to write about the ancestral land from a removed but impassioned viewpoint, but we can also write about the land we happen to be citizens of with the same gaze, holding up a mirror to the very place we are "exiled," discovering new identities in the process of our writing. However, can we really call second and third generation Palestinians and, in many cases, part-Palestinians, exiles?

Exile can take many forms—from the logistical (due to occupation and civil war) and the political (at odds with the powers that be), to the cultural (those Americans in Paris again) and even spiritual (abandonment of faith). Some of these are easier to redress than others, and some may actually be desirable. But how does this relate to Palestine or, as the title of this anthology has it, seeking Palestine? To be literal-minded about it, and according to the dictionary definition, I and millions of others born in diaspora outside historic Palestine are not exiles. We have not, ourselves, been expelled. Yes, we have been prohibited from returning to live.

But again, if you have never lived there, then you cannot, literally speaking, "return," even if you were allowed to.[5] So what does this mean in reality? And if it is inaccurate to call those born to exiles, exiles, what do we call them? Let me make it clear that I am not trivialising the dream of "returning home" after two generations; I am exploring the language we use when talking about it. It is a cliché to say that words are our weapons, but they are, and we need to use them with a forensic accuracy not possible with real weapons.

Exile, as we have seen, is the forced expulsion from (or voluntary leaving of) one's country or homeland. But what has happened to all Palestinians in diaspora (not just those born outside) is not simply their expulsion, but the gradual dismantling of their abandoned homeland. Our parents and grandparents were displaced from Palestine, their villages bulldozed, the land remodeled and reconstructed into something else, a homeland to suit someone else. What hasn't been fully incorporated into this new entity is occupied by force or, as in the case of Gaza, turned into a giant prison. Every effort has been made to make it disappear, to remove it from the map of our consciousness, including the building of a towering wall over which it is impossible to see. Descendants of Palestinians bearing the passports of their country of birth are fortunate if they are issued tourist visas to visit this quickly dissolving place. We have been reduced to tourists visiting the ongoing disfiguration of the ancestral landscape. We have been dispossessed, not exiled. Something has been stolen and disguised so that it is no longer recognizable. We have become rootless, citizens of the world.

Perhaps, in the future, we will be performing a Palestinian version of the Jewish *aliyah*,[6] which Arabs will call "the return" or some such, and descendants of Palestinians from all over the globe will be claiming it as their spiritual homeland. When that happens, I don't know how many would take it up—it is, after all, an entitlement we are talking about, not an obligation. Those who do go may build new communities to replace ancestral villages erased by Zionist dreamers, perhaps even demolishing Jewish settlements built on the hills of the West Bank in the process,[7] and replacing the displacing tribe. I am willing to bet that these returnees will come to be known as "outsiders" or "tourists" by Palestinians already living there, and derided when they don't give up their foreign passports.[8] And who would blame them? Those of us in diaspora not living in refugee camps live in relative peace and affluence, free of the daily humiliations and brutal crackdown to which those under the Occupation are subject—an Occupation that protects the expanding "realities on the ground," a disingenuous phrase which evokes an unavoidable act of nature rather than a deliberate policy of tribal settlement.

It is an accident of time and place and people that we are in the situation we are in, and we cannot be blamed for that. Yet, that doesn't stop some of us from feeling slightly fraudulent making judgements about the struggle for Palestinian nationalism from afar. However, we are entitled to do just that, as the struggle is taking place everywhere, although in different forms, on various fronts and with varying agendas. Those living outside are entitled, for instance, to use our dislocated perspective to question the efforts by the Palestinian Authority to seek international recognition of this increasingly cantonized place as a Palestinian State. We are allowed to say that we think it a token gesture that panders to a fixation with statehood, and although it might give a psychological boost to occupied Palestinians, it will do little to change their reality. And we are even more entitled to speak out when it is confirmed that a Palestinian state is unlikely to include millions of us living outside.[9]

Nor is a call for freedom meaningful. Freedom from what? Occupation, yes, of course. But freedom *to do* what? Rosa Luxemburg, herself described by the prosecutor in her trial as "a creature without a home," famously spoke of how freedom is always the freedom to think otherwise. And this is where your freedom-fighting bedfellows with whom you shared a dream of liberation can become your enemies: when you realize that all they wanted was the freedom to exploit and oppress you themselves.

So something more fundamental is needed, something that is not about bordered states or flags or rousing national anthems or having a currency with your national heroes on it or being able to parade your army on independence day. If truth be told, I want no part of such a place—those things are not an identity, they are a state. I need something bigger-hearted and more inclusive. Something that looks for commonality rather than difference. I am, of course, talking about universal humanism. Human rights. Two words that cause eyes to glaze over and hearts to sink. Words that have become trivialized. But these are phrases to reclaim for everyday applicability: for instance, the right of return for those of us who want it, the right to travel on the same roads as someone from another religion, to build a house, to have access to the same resources, to believe or not believe in god, etc. Universal rights means giving up privileges that have to be held onto with brute force because they are at the expense of others. I am talking about all-embracing ideals to be adopted by everyone living in Palestine and Israel, never mind their ethnic origin or religion, and indeed all of us living outside Palestine whose ancestors were born there. Palestine is destined (or doomed, depending on your point of view) to be the spiritual and religious home to many people of varying faiths (including the faithless) and of differing ethnic origins, and should be celebrated as such without preference being given to one or the other. To paraphrase Hannah Arendt, a place "in which a universal humanity and a genuine, almost naive contempt for social and ethnic distinctions are taken for granted." I realize I am describing a somewhat utopian fantasy world and that the reality, when (not if) it comes about, will undoubtedly be a pale shadow of what I mean.

But this in essence is what binds us all together. It is the golden thread that not just ties us back to Palestine but *pulls us forward* to a new one. As the Greek tragedy that is Zionism crashes into its third act and its *hamartia*[10] leads to its inevitable self-destruction, it is still desperately removing traces of Palestine as it used to be. In the meantime, we try to undo the damage by passing on histories, doing the embroidery, cooking the food, mapping destroyed villages, and generally keeping the history alive—all of which is necessary, but without becoming trapped in history. Because Palestine can never (and should not) be redrawn to look like it was before Israel, and Hassan Hijazi, when he manages to make it back to Jaffa permanently, will not be returning to the same place in which his parents were born. But that hardly matters. We can only move forwards, not backwards. We are already re-imagining a Palestine that reflects who we are now and who we hope to become. In time, hopefully, it will prevail.

However, when that happens, I reserve the right to graduate from being dispossessed to becoming an exile.

### Notes

1 Estimates vary, but there are approximately 4.5 million people born to Palestinian refugees and their descendants in the diaspora since 1948, and no more than 4 percent of Palestinians alive today were born before 1948.

2 I am referring to those born or displaced outside historic Palestine. Those displaced within Palestine (and their offspring) are still under Occupation, and therefore cannot be free to get on with their lives. Nor indeed can those living in refugee camps in Lebanon, Syria and Jordan.

3 Again, I exclude people living in refugee camps. According to UNRWA, more than 1.4 million Palestinians are currently living in fifty-eight camps.

4 Lebanon's political system and government are still divided along sectarian grounds.

5 This does not prevent Jews all over the world from "returning" to Palestine, where they believe they originated thousands of years ago. They are welcomed with open arms, whereas those whose parents and grandparents were born there are excluded because they happen to be from the wrong tribe.

6 *Aliyah*, a Hebrew word which means ascent or going up, is an important Jewish concept. According to Jewish tradition, traveling to the "Land of Israel" is an ascent, both geographically and metaphysically. *Aliyah* is enshrined in Israel's Law of Return. (*Source: Wikipedia*)

7 It has to be said that many of these places should be removed on aesthetic grounds alone, since they are so obviously alien to the landscape.

[8] Just as Jews performing *aliyah* apparently hold on to their original citizenships, in case the spiritual homeland doesn't live up to its touted promise.

[9] Revelations in the so-called Palestine Papers, which exposed the reality of negotiations between Israel and the Palestinian Authority, show that any right of return for those in diaspora is unlikely to be included in any final settlement.

[10] Referred to in Aristotle's *Poetics* as the character's flaw or mistake that leads to their downfall in a tragedy.

# KARMA NABULSI

## Exiled from Revolution

In recent years, when young Palestinian activists
meet up with veterans of the Palestinian struggle, they show us—the
generation of the revolution—an unexpected thoughtfulness and
patience. These often silent gestures are nothing like the traditional
courtesies typically extended to an older generation in our part of
the world, nor the calm certainty those inheriting power sometimes
show towards those losing it. They are more intimate and more
poignant. What brings us together is always the need to discuss the
options before us and to see if a plan can be made. Everyone argues,
laughs, shouts and tells dark jokes. But whenever a proper discussion
begins, the suddenly lowered voices of our frustrated young people,
many of them at the heart of fierce protests on university campuses
and in rights campaigns elsewhere, have the same tone I used to
hear in the voices of our young ambulance workers in Lebanon in
the 1970s and 1980s: an elegiac gentleness towards the hopelessly
wounded, towards those who were already beyond repair.

Today, the way Palestinians see things, the fragmentation of the
body politic—externally engineered and increasingly internally
driven—has now been achieved. Even the liberal Israeli press has
begun to notice that the key people in Ramallah, the Palestinian
Authority's capital in the West Bank, no longer discuss strategies of
liberation but rather the huge business deals that prey on the public

imagination. Every institution or overarching structure that once united Palestinians has now crumbled and been swept away. The gulf between Gaza and the West Bank, between Hamas and Fatah, between Palestinians inside Palestine and the millions of refugees outside it, between city and village, town and refugee camp, now seems unbridgeable. The elites are tiny and the numbers of the dispossessed and the disenfranchised increase every day. There is, at this moment, no single body able to claim legitimately to represent all Palestinians, no body able to set out a collective policy or national program of liberation. There is no plan.

The feeling of paralysis doesn't affect only the Palestinians. It is found, too, among the hundreds of international institutions and less formal groups involved in the thriving carpetbagging industry of the Middle East Peace Process. Over the last decade, these bodies have produced thousands of institutional memos, governmental reports, official démarches, human rights briefings, summaries, analyses, legal inquiries into war crimes and human rights abuses, academic books and articles. And they have pretty much nailed it: Palestinians are enduring the entrenched effects not only of a military occupation, but of a colonial regime that practices apartheid.

The predicament is understood and widely accepted, yet Palestinians and non-Palestinians appear equally baffled. Protest and denunciation have achieved very little. How are we to respond in a way that will allow us to prevail? The vocabulary required to form a policy is entirely absent both nationally and internationally. Palestinians are currently trapped in a historical moment that—as the contemporary world sees it—belongs to the past. The language the situation demands had life only inside an ideology which has now disappeared.

Everyone else has moved on. In a world whose intellectual framework is derived from university courses in postcolonial or cultural studies, from the discourse of post-nationalism or human rights or global governance, from post-conflict and security literature, the Palestinians are stuck fast in historical amber. They can't move on, and the language that could assist them to do so is as extinct as Aramaic. No one cares any longer for talk of liberation: in fact, people flinch at the sound of it—it is unfashionable, embarrassing, reactionary even, to speak of revolution today. Twenty-first century eyes read revolutionary engagement as the first stage on the road to the guillotine or the Gulag. Seen through this prism, Palestinians remain stubbornly—one could almost say, wilfully—in the anti-colonial, revolutionary phase of their history.

If you raise the painful subject of this earlier time among Palestinians today, the usual effect is to revive the over-theoretical debate about when exactly the revolution died. (A discussion of its strengths and weaknesses would be more useful.) Some say it ended after Black September in Jordan in 1970; others that it ended in 1975 at the start of the Lebanese civil war. The majority see Israel's invasion of Lebanon in 1982, which brought about the comprehensive destruction of the PLO's infrastructure, as having killed it off. The communiqués and declarations issued during the First Intifada, which took place in the Occupied Palestinian Territories between 1987 and 1993, were expressed in the language of revolution, but everyone agrees that it was all over by 1991, when the Madrid peace process was accepted on such unequal terms. That entire period of Palestinian history has fallen into disrepute for a number of reasons—not least having to watch its ghoulish remains driving around in official cars in Ramallah or posing at the White House—so the benefits are never assessed, or potentially useful lessons drawn.

Palestinians old enough to remember such things commonly agree that we are currently at a collective nadir in a long history of resistance. The only sign of forward movement lies within the tide of concerted revulsion for Israel's belligerent policies, which Palestinian civil society organizations have directed into a vivid and well-organized campaign of solidarity with the Palestinian people through boycott, divestment and sanctions.

One enlightening precedent for this dismal situation can be found in recent Palestinian political history. Exactly fifty years ago,

189

Palestinians were at a similar stage of institutional, social and political fragmentation, jammed into the in-between of defeat, dispossession and anomie resulting from the forced dispersal of the majority of people into neighboring countries after the Nakba of 1948. Unprotected by a sovereign state, without a country, facing Israel and various Arab regimes that controlled every aspect of social and civic life as well as physical space, deep in the dust, mud and disease of cities made from tents, without papers or property; by 1960 the political fragmentation was complete. That year a young Palestinian writer, Ghassan Kanafani, moved to Kuwait from Syria, where he had been a teacher at a school set up for refugees by the UN, after himself being expelled from Palestine in 1948 with his family. One of the most prescient chroniclers of his people's spirit, he described the current mood in his diary:

> The only thing that we know is that tomorrow will be no better than today, and that we are waiting on the banks, yearning, for a boat that will not come. We are sentenced to be separated from everything—except from our own destruction.[1]

But what appeared to Kanafani like the collective end was instead its extraordinary beginning. In reply to the intolerable pressure of empty space, the revolution found form and words and action on such a scale that, for the first time in nearly a century of rebellions and uprisings against foreign rule, Palestinians landed upon the right mechanism to overcome international, Israeli and Arab coercion, and unify sufficiently in order to represent themselves. The history of Palestinian attempts to achieve freedom would give anyone pause: two generations of its work lie buried in the cemeteries of over two dozen countries. For Palestinians, whose national politics were undone in an instant over a single year in 1948, only the concerted actions of tens of thousands of cadres right across the region was a strong enough glue to hold people together while putting sufficient pressure on foreign governments and their agencies intent upon forcing us to accommodate to an Israel bent on our destruction.

The overall sensibility of that short period was, against all expectations, profoundly popular and democratic: pluralist, multi-party, universalist, secular and highly progressive. Palestinians who dared not join—businessmen, academics, the predatory classes—were carried bustling along in its powerful wake, and obeyed its popular mandate. Today we could not be further from that fleeting instance of unity the Palestinian revolution once afforded.

It is revolutionaries who make revolutions, and not the other way around. During the national mobilization of the 1960s and 1970s, some joined the party, others the movement, but most simply joined the Palestinian revolution. It was taken for granted that one belonged to one of the parties, which were themselves embedded in the broader national liberation movement under the umbrella of the Palestine Liberation Organization, a formal institution set up in 1964 by Arab states, which was captured from the Palestinian elite by the resistance groups a few years later. Empowered by becoming part of a fast-moving popular revolution, Palestinians—exiled, scattered and defeated as they were—achieved the two elusive things they have constantly sought: representation and unity.

The experience of revolutionary life is difficult to describe. It is as much metaphysical as imaginative, combining urgency, purposefulness, seriousness and hard work, with a nearcelebratory sense of adventure and overriding optimism: a sort of carnival atmosphere of citizens' rule. Key to its success is that this heightened state is consciously and collectively maintained by tens of thousands of people at the same time. If you get tired for a few hours or days, you know others are holding the ring. One could therefore, and on a daily basis, witness the most creative political episodes—in the way people looked or spoke or lived their lives, but especially in their ability to constantly fashion what would normally be considered (in circumstances of more regular wartime experiences), impossible acts. Young Palestinians feel unable to touch these almost fairytale stories of their own history

191

that seem, in their grinding daily struggles, utterly out of reach. When trying to conceptualize (or simply understand) what those of the generation of the revolution actually did and how on earth they did it, one familiar textbook signpost might be the commanding role Lenin bequeaths the vanguard, the necessary few who lead. Yet the model that emerges from Palestinian history, drawing on a century of rebellions and uprisings, is radically different in its formulation, and more closely mirrors the dozens of such revolutions to establish democracies in nineteenth century Europe: the acts of a few are matched, and then rapidly overtaken, by an entire nation of people, all of whom consider themselves leaders, as equals. No one here waits around for instructions. In the meantime, in our period of seeming paralysis, in what appear to many as random and foolish acts, Palestinian individuals and small associations keep striking that match, hoping that this is the moment for things to take.

The Arab revolutions of 2011 have recently opened the road for a return to Palestinian organizing of this kind to once again be truly collective, to reclaim its real tradition, for they highlight that self-same, single principle large enough to unify and return us into the revolutionary present we have been waiting and working for these past decades. Popular sovereignty's foundational nature means that every time its principle is collectively asserted or re-asserted, we possess the right to shape our destiny far beyond that of voting for a party or for an individual, or the right to read about the things people do in our names in the newspaper. This fundamental freedom means we shape the very institutions that represent us, that they actually belong to us.

The awestruck West watches mesmerized, over this spring and summer, as masses of Arabs—displaying all the virtues of free citizens—create and celebrate their revolutions with such breathtaking energy and beauty across the Arab world: everyone can catch its glory and everyone can immediately recognize it as a familiar joy, the most precious of our collective possessions. Popular sovereignty's fresh enactment returns to each citizen the gift of collective spirit—a spirit that resides within each individual. In everyday terms, this public freedom can best be imagined as the public square in any of our cities. In the square the presence of popular sovereignty is much more visible and recognizable to the naked eye: without a roof, open to the heavens, the workings of the democratic body politic can easily be appreciated for the stuff it is made of. How does the public square get recreated and reclaimed by citizens and, just as important, how is it held once it is recaptured, once we return to our busy daily affairs? Cairo's Maidan al-Tahrir, Liberation Square, was filled day after day with the multitude, the mass, the collective spirit of the nation. This made it, of course, a revolutionary gesture, as popular sovereignty could clearly be seen to lie with them, and not with the army or the police or the dictator, all of whom had a firm grip on the recognized instruments of state. Yet this sovereign citizenry was not comprised of a spontaneous outpouring of a massed multitude of individuals. For well over a decade before the public square became filled with ordinary citizens, the square itself was fought for, inch by inch, year after year, increasingly held and finally won by a vast assortment of politically organized civic associations of different sizes and histories.

One of the individuals who still keeps the revolutionary spirit alive in these bleak times for Palestine phoned me a while ago, and this time I rang him back. Ziyad was a key activist in the First Intifada when he was a student at Birzeit University in the West Bank, and for the last twenty years he has dedicated his life in Gaza to what is commonly known as "mobilizing from below." Ziyad is, or was, head of the Rafah refugee camp's popular committee, the local elected body, legendary now for its history of civic resistance to Israeli rule. Ziyad is like an artist, restlessly exploring ways to preserve people's humanity amid the oppression and misery of southern Gaza. His cool eye and steady nerve, together with a seemingly inexhaustible affection for others, have kept him from turning away in despair at the things he has seen. At the height of the war on Gaza, he managed to create and sustain the only committee that included all the factions, with Fatah members working alongside Hamas or vice versa. Members of other committees who had previously tried this (including his own) had been kneecapped for their pains.

Ziyad spent much of 2009 in prison in Gaza and, as it turned out when I returned his call, some of the next year's Ramadan as well. "Oh no!" I said, "What happened this time?" He said that he'd been trying to organize in the elementary schools. This struck me as one of the funniest things I had heard in a long time; Ziyad laughed, too, when he began telling me about it. He had tried to organize a prize-giving in the camp for some of the students, but the current administration in Gaza didn't like the idea at all. "We are not selecting children from Hamas families or Fatah families," he said, "just those who had done well in school. We had to try something!"

What the administration in Gaza does not like, Ziyad said, is the idea of movement, of freedom, of opening things up from below, of bringing people together for any common purpose at all. I told him I had spoken to Adnan in Beirut only that morning, and that the story was no different there: Adnan had been forced to stay at home for months, unable to move. Until two years ago, he had worked closely with another old friend of mine, Kamal Medhat, a child of the revolution who was not so different from Ziyad in his determination to go it alone while carrying everyone with him.

Just over two years ago, Kamal was assassinated by a car bomb in south Lebanon. He had been trying to urge people forward towards national unity, and to attack the political corruption then entrenched in the refugee camps: these two objectives, it soon became clear, were intertwined. He was making a very successful job of it, for he brought formidable experience to the task. Already a legend as a young man, Kamal was responsible for, among many other things, the security of the leadership when the revolution was centered in Beirut and attempts against it took place on an almost daily basis. An obituary in the Arab press noted that, "he constantly criticized Arafat, who would laugh." This was true: Kamal could be brutally honest, but he made everyone in the room feel happy, taking and giving endless orders, joking, and being especially encouraging to young cadres, though also quite tough. I witnessed at least a dozen acts of bravery by Kamal in the 1970s and early 1980s. After the PLO leadership was evacuated to Tunis in 1982, he returned to Lebanon to help lift the military siege of the Palestinian refugee camps by the Syrians and their proxies. In the 1990s, in disagreement with the leadership's negotiating strategy, he absented himself from public life, studying for a doctorate in international law, staying very quiet. We lost track of each other until a few years ago when he burst back onto the scene in Lebanon, unchanged and undefeated, now the second-in-command at the PLO embassy that had finally been re-established there.

I went to his funeral; we all walked the familiar path to the Palestinian cemetery, accompanied by thousands of refugees, clapping and singing and shouting revolutionary slogans. After the forty days of mourning, I returned to Beirut, where the traditional memorial meeting was convened at the UNESCO palace. The hall was packed with Palestinians from the refugee camps across Lebanon, and black and white images of the handsome Kamal at different stages of his life succeeded one another on a screen behind the stage. Most of the Palestinian leaders were at an urgent meeting in Amman, and couldn't attend. The eerie pockets of silence at various moments throughout the ceremony were bound up, it seemed to me, with the implications of his death (don't organize, don't push, don't try to change things for the better). Something felt as if it was about to give.

Afterwards, in the foyer, a stream of young people came up to me. They wanted me to know exactly what he had meant to them: "Kamal was the only one who spoke up for us"; "Kamal listened to us, he stood with us"; "He fought for us"; "He encouraged us." One after another they told me stories of what he did. Each had recognized his revolutionary spirit, I thought, as I watched them wander away afterwards into the streets of Beirut.

It had done its work, and lit a match.

**Note**

¹ Ghassan Kanafani, "Diary Excerpts 1959–62," *Al Carmel* (Spring 1981).

*An earlier version of this essay was published in the* London Review of Books *on October 21, 2010. We thank the* LRB *and editor Mary-Kay Wilmers for permission to reproduce it.*

# Contributors

**Lila Abu-Lughod**, a Palestinian-American, is the Joseph L. Buttenwieser Professor of Social Science at Columbia University where she teaches anthropology and women's and gender studies. She has authored or edited a number of award-winning books including *Veiled Sentiments: Honor and Poetry in a Bedouin Society* (1986); *Writing Women's Worlds* (1993); *Remaking Women: Feminism and Modernity in the Middle East* (1998); *Dramas of Nationhood: The Politics of Television in Egypt* (2005); and *Nakba: Palestine, 1948, and the Claims of Memory* (2007).

**Susan Abulhawa** is the author of the international bestseller, *Mornings in Jenin* (2010), and contributing author to anthologies. Abulhawa's essays have appeared in major print and online media throughout the world. She is a frequent speaker and political commentator, and is the founder of Playgrounds for Palestine, a children's nonprofit NGO dedicated to upholding The Right to Play for Palestinian children in the Occupied Territories and in refugee camps elsewhere.

**Suad Amiry** is an architect and writer. She is the founder of Riwaq, the Center for Architectural Conservation, in Ramallah. Amiry is the author of *Sharon and My Mother-in-Law* (2005), which won the prestigious Italian literary prize, Viareggio

(2004). Recent books include *Menopausal Palestine* (Women Unlimited, 2010) and *Nothing to Lose But Your Life* (2010). Amiry was a member of the Palestinian Delegation to the Washington Peace Talks (1991–1993). She is married to Salim Tamari and lives in Ramallah.

**Rana Barakat** is an assistant professor at the Department of Philosophy and Cultural Studies and the Graduate Program of Contemporary Arab Studies at Birzeit University. After spending a year and a half away from Palestine, she is currently teaching at Birzeit once again. Barakat works on various issues including revolutionary social movements, the history of Jerusalem, contemporary Arab history, and colonialism and its postcolonial resonance in the Palestinian cultural sphere. She is currently co-editing a book about pseudo-transitional Palestine at the turn of the new century, and also working on a manuscript that deals with the social and political transitions of her specific definition of Jerusalem in the Mandate period, with a primary focus on the western corridor and the urban *fallah*.

**Mourid Barghouti** was born in 1944 in the West Bank village of Deir Ghassaneh. His most recent book is *I Was Born There, I Was Born Here* (2011). He has published thirteen books of poetry in Arabic including a *Collected Works* (1997), and received the Palestine Award for poetry in 2000. His memoir, *I Saw Ramallah* (1997), translated by Ahdaf Soueif, received widespread critical acclaim. A selection of his poetry, *Midnight and Other Poems*, was published in English in 2008. He lives in Cairo with his wife, the novelist and critic Radwa Ashour.

**Beshara Doumani**, professor of history at the University of California, Berkeley, is the author of *Rediscovering Palestine: Merchants and Peasants of Jabal Nablus, 1700–1900* (1995); and editor of *Family History in the Middle East: Household, Property, and Gender* (2003) and *Academic Freedom after September 11* (2006). His book, *The Rightful Heirs: Family Law and Islamic Law in Ottoman Syria 1660–1860*, is forthcoming.

**Sharif S. Elmusa** is a widely published poet, environmental scholar and literary translator. He was born in the village of Al-Abbasiyya, ten miles from the city of Jaffa. The village was the second largest of more than four hundred villages depopulated and largely destroyed by Israel in 1948. He grew up in the refugee camp of Al-Nuwayma, on the outskirts of the town of Jericho in the West Bank. Elmusa received his undergraduate degree from Cairo University and his doctorate from the Massachusetts Institute of Technology. He wrote *Flawed Landscape: Poems 1987–2008* (2008) and co-edited the pioneering anthology, *Grape Leaves: A Century of Arab-American Poetry* (1988). He is the author of *Water Conflict: Economics, Politics, Law and the Palestinian–Israeli Water Resources* (1997); and editor of *Culture and the Natural Environment: Ancient and Modern Middle Eastern Texts* (2005) and *The Burden of Resources: Oil and Water Wars in the Gulf and Nile Basin* (2011). His own poems, essays and translations of Arabic poetry have appeared in numerous publications. Since 1999, he has been associate professor of political science at the American University in Cairo, except for two years at Georgetown University in Qatar (2009–11). His poetry manuscript, *Should You Wish to Stay: Poems from Cairo*, is looking for a home.

**Rema Hammami** was born in Saudi Arabia and grew up in Jerusalem, Britain, Belgium and the US. In 1987 she returned to Jerusalem, which continues to be her home. A professor of anthropology at Birzeit University, she has written widely on various aspects of gender, nationalism, Palestinian society and politics. She is co-translator, with John Berger, of Mahmoud Darwish's epic poem, *Mural* (2009).

**Mischa Hiller**, who is of Palestinian and English descent, was born in the UK. He has lived in England, Lebanon and Tanzania. He is the author of *Sabra Zoo* (2010), a novel set against the backdrop of the 1982 Sabra and Shatila massacres in Beirut, and *Shake Off* (2011), about a survivor of the events in *Sabra Zoo* who is recruited as an undercover PLO agent in Europe. He currently lives in England with his wife and children.

Emily Jacir's images open each section of this anthology. Her work spans a diverse range of media and strategies including film, photography, social interventions, installation, performance, video, writing and sound. Recurrent themes in her practice include repressed historical narratives, resistance, political land divisions, movement (both forced and voluntary), and the logic of the archive. Jacir has shown extensively throughout Europe, the Americas and the Middle East since 1994. Recent awards include a Golden Lion at the 52$^{nd}$ Venice Biennale (2007) for her work, *Material for a Film*; a Prince Claus Award from the Prince Claus Fund in The Hague (2007); and the Hugo Boss Prize at the Guggenheim Museum (2008). *Belongings*, a monograph on a selection of Jacir's work from 1998 to 2003, was published in 2003; her second monograph was published in 2008. She has been actively involved in education in Palestine since 2000, including at PIVF and Birzeit University. She is a full-time professor at the International Academy of Art, Palestine, where she has been teaching since 2006. She is the Resident Artist at the Home Workspace Program, Beirut (2011–2012). She conceived of and co-curated the first Palestine International Video Festival in Ramallah in 2002. She also curated a selection of shorts, *Palestinian Revolution Cinema* (1968–1982), which went on tour in 2007.

Penny Johnson is an independent researcher who works closely with the Institute of Women's Studies at Birzeit University, where she edits the *Review of Women's Studies*. Johnson's recent writing and research on Palestine has focused on weddings and wars, wives of political prisoners, and young Palestinians' talk about proper and improper marriages. She is an associate editor of the *Jerusalem Quarterly* and lives in Ramallah.

Fady Joudah, a Palestinian–American physician, won the Yale Series for Younger Poets in 2007 for his collection, *The Earth in the Attic*. His translations of Mahmoud Darwish's poetry have won a TLS/Banipal prize from the UK in 2008 and a PEN USA prize in 2010. He is also the translator of Ghassan Zaqtan's poetry,

*Like a Straw Bird It Follows Me* (2012). Joudah's second collection, *Alight*, is forthcoming (2013).

**Jean Said Makdisi** was born in Jerusalem and grew up in Cairo, where she completed her secondary education. She then moved to the US for her university studies and began her married life there, returning to Beirut with her husband and three sons in 1972. Today an independent writer and researcher, she taught English and humanities at the Beirut University College (presently the Lebanese American University) from 1972 until 1995. During that time she also worked in the university theater, writing and directing. She is a member and twice secretary general of the Lebanese Association of Women Researchers *(bahithat)*, with whom she co-organized and participated in several conferences and co-edited several books. She is the author of *Beirut Fragments: A War Memoir* (1990), which was selected as a *New York Times* Notable Book, 1990, and *Teta, Mother and Me: Three Generations of Arab Women* (2005). She also edited *Jerusalem Memories* by Serene Husseini Shahid (2000) and co-edited the English language version of *My Life in the PLO* by Shafiq al Hout (2011).

**Karma Nabulsi** lectures at Oxford University and is Fellow in Politics at St Edmund Hall. She is the author of a number of works on eighteenth-century political thought, nineteenth-century revolutionary republicanism and the construction of democratic republics, the laws of war, and the politics of Palestinian refugees and democracy. She is director of the *Civitas* collective project on civic rights and needs of Palestinian refugees and exiles, and editor of its register, *Palestinians Register: Laying Foundations and Setting Directions*. She is Chair of Trustees of the HOPING Foundation, which supports art and education for young Palestinian refugees and their associations in refugee camps across the Arab world.

**Raeda Sa'adeh**, who contributed the image on the cover of this book, was born in Um El Fahem in 1977, and received her BFA and MFA from Bezalel Academy of Arts and

Design in Jerusalem. She was the winner of the first Young Artist of the Year Award organized by the A M Qattan Foundation in 2000. Her work in photography, performance and video has been exhibited widely in Europe and the US. Recent exhibitions include "Re-Orientations" at the European Parliament, Brussels; "No Man's Land" at the GEMAK Museum, The Hague; "In Transit" at the House of World Cultures, Berlin; and "Biennal Cuvee" at the OK Center, Lens. Sa'adeh's work was included in the Sydney Biennial (2006) and the Sharjah Biennial (2007). She lives and works in Jerusalem.

Raja Shehadeh, a Palestinian lawyer and writer living in Ramallah, won the Orwell Prize in 2008 for *Palestinian Walks: Notes on a Vanishing Landscape.* An author of several books on international law and Palestinian human rights under Israeli military occupation, he has published a number of memoirs, including *Strangers in the House* (2002) and *When the Bulbul Stopped Singing* (2003), which became a successful stage play. *A Rift in Time: Travels with my Ottoman Uncle* was published in 2011 and *Occupation Diaries* was published in 2012.

Adania Shibli is the author of two novels, *Touch* and *We Are All Equally Far from Love,* many short stories and narrative and art essays, which have appeared in various anthologies, art books and magazines. She has twice won the Qattan Young Writer's Award-Palestine: in 2001, for her novel *Masaas* and in 2003, for her novel *Kulluna Ba'id Bethat al Miqdar 'an el-Hub.* In addition, Shibli is engaged in academic writing and research. In 2009, she gained a PhD in media and cultural studies from the University of East London. She is currently a post-doctoral fellow at the Wissenschaftskolleg Zu Berlin, EUME program.